Emblems of our Messianic Jewish Faith in Messiah Yeshua

From the Heart of the Rabbis Vol. 12

DMM Publishing
Teaching Torah Truth In Messiah Yeshua

Rabbin Deborah Brandt

Copyright 2016

Table of Contents

I. The Land of Israel

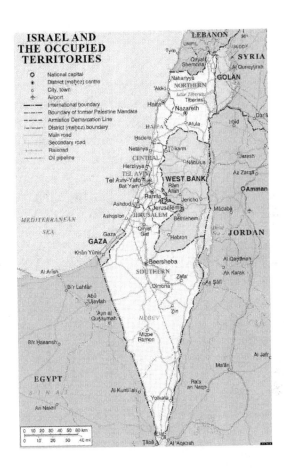

II.   The Menorah

One of the oldest symbols of the Jewish faith is the menorah, a seven-branched candelabrum used in the Temple.

It has been said that the menorah is a symbol of the nation of Israel and its mission to be "a light unto the nations." (Isaiah 42:6). The sages emphasize that light is not a violent force; Israel is to accomplish its mission by setting an example, not by using force. This idea is highlighted in the vision of the Prophet Zechariah who sees a menorah, and G-d explains: "Not by might, nor by power, but by My spirit." (Zechariah 4:1-6)

The kohanim lit the menorah in the Sanctuary every evening and cleaned it out every morning, replacing the wicks and putting fresh olive oil into the cups. The illustration featured on this page is based on instructions for construction of the menorah found in Exodus 25:31-40.

The lamp stand in today's synagogues, called the ner tamid (lit. the continual lamp; usually translated as the eternal flame), symbolizes the menorah.

The nine-branched menorah used on Chanukah is commonly patterned after this menorah, because Chanukah commemorates the miracle that a day's worth of oil for this menorah lasted eight days.

The menorah in the First and Second Temples had seven branches. After the Temples were destroyed, a tradition developed not to duplicate anything from the Temple and therefore menorah's no longer had seven branches. The use of six-branched menorahs became popular, but, in modern times, some rabbis have gone back to the seven-branched menorahs, arguing that they are not the same as those used in the Temple because today's are electrified.[1]

---

[1] Judaism 101

III. Kiddush Cup

What is The Kiddush Cup?

The Kiddush cup is a beautifully decorated wine vessel through which and into which the blessing comes. Kiddush, meaning sanctification, is the prayer recited over a cup of wine in the home and synagogue on the eve of the Sabbath, festivals, weddings, Bar/Bat Mitzvah, Bris and baby naming before the start of the meal.

The Kiddush praises God while reciting the blessing over wine while looking at the wine itself.

Baruch atah Adonai, Eloheinu Melech *ha'olam,* borei *p'ri ha'gafen*
Blessed are you, Lord our God, Ruler of the universe, who creates the fruit of the vine.

Kiddush cups can be made of sterling silver, silver plate, pewter, fine china or pottery. Some are artfully crafted of other materials. Kiddush cups have always been elaborately designed and may display one's family emblem, Jerusalem, Shabbat prayers, or an engraved name and date.

The Kiddush cup is filled with wine and placed on the palm of the right hand so the cup is held by the upturned fingers. The palm corresponds to the letter yud, and the five fingers correspond to the letter hay, an allusion to these first two letters of Yud Hey name.

IV.   Torah Scroll[2]

A Torah Scroll is the holiest book within Judaism, made up of the five books of Moses.

• There are 304,805 letters in a Torah Scroll.

• Each page has 42 lines.

• The Torah Scroll must be written by a specially trained pious scribe called a *sofer*.

• A *sofer* must know more than 4,000 Judaic laws before he begins writing a Torah Scroll.

• It takes about a year to write an entire Torah Scroll.

• Even a single missing or misshapen letter invalidates the entire Sefer Torah.

• The Torah we use today in your synagogue is written exactly the same way the Torah was written the very first time by Moses 3,300 years ago.

• The Torah is made of many sheets of parchment that are sewn together to make one very long scroll.

• The entire Torah is written by hand, each letter is inscribed and individually formed with a quill and specially prepared ink.

• The Torah is read at least four times a week in synagogues around the world.

---

2 Torah Scroll Facts By <u>Dovid Zaklikowski</u>

V.   Yod/Yad

Beyond its practical usage in pointing out letters, the yad ensures that the parchment is not touched during the reading. There are several reasons for this: handling the parchment renders one ritually impure and the often-fragile parchment is easily damaged. Moreover, the vellum parchment does not absorb ink so touching the scroll with fingers will damage the lettering.[1] While not required when chanting from the Torah, it is used frequently and is considered a *hidur mitzvah* ("embellishment of the commandment") of reading the Torah.

VI. Kippah

Kippah (pronounced kee-pah) is the Hebrew word for the skullcap traditionally worn by Jewish men. It is also called a yarmulke or koppel in Yiddish. Kippot (plural of kippah) are worn at the apex of a person's head. After the Star of David, they are probably one of the most recognizable symbols of Jewish identity.

Who Wears Kippot and When?

Traditionally only Jewish men wore kippot. However, in modern times some women also choose to wear kippot as an expression of their Jewish identity or as a form of religious expression.

When a kippah is worn varies from person to person. In Orthodox circles Jewish men usually wear kippot all the time, whether they are attending a religious service or going about their daily lives outside of the synagogue. In Conservative communities men almost always wear kippot during religious services or during formal occasions, such as during a High Holiday dinner or when attending a Bar Mitzvah. In Reform circles, it is equally common for men to wear kippot as it is for them not to wear kippot.

Ultimately the decision about whether or not to wear a kippah comes down to personal choice and the customs of the community an individual belongs to. Religiously speaking, wearing kippot is not obligatory and there are many Jewish men who do not wear them at all.

What Does a Kippah Look Like?

Originally all kippot looked the same. They were small, black skullcaps worn at the apex of a man's head. However, nowadays kippot come in all sorts of colors and sizes. Visit your local Judaica shop or a market in Jerusalem and you will see everything from knitted kippot in all the colors of the rainbow to kippot sporting baseball team logos. Some kippot will be small skullcaps, others will cover the entire head, and yet others will resemble caps. When women wear kippot sometimes they select ones made of lace or that are adorned with feminine decorations. Both men and women usually attach kippot to their hair with bobby pins.

Among those who wear kippot, it is not uncommon to have a collection of different styles, colors and sizes. This variety allows the wearer to select whichever kippah suits their mood or their reason for wearing it. For instance, a black kippah might be worn to a funeral, while a colorful kippah might be worn to a holiday gathering. When a Jewish boy has a Bar Mitzvah or a Jewish girl has a Bat Mitzvah, oftentimes special kippot will be made for the occasion.

Why Do Jews Wear Kippot?

Wearing a kippah is not a religious commandment. Rather it is a Jewish custom that over time has come to be associated with Jewish identity and showing respect for God. In Orthodox and Conservative circles covering one's head is seen as a sign of *yirat Shamayim*, which means "reverence for God" in Hebrew. This concept comes from the Talmud, where wearing a head covering is associated with showing respect for God and for men of higher social status. Some scholars also cite the Middle Age custom of covering one's head in the presence of royalty. Since God is the "King of Kings" it made sense to also cover one's head during prayer or religious services, when one hopes to approach the Divine through worship.

According to author Alfred Koltach, the earliest reference to a Jewish head covering comes from Exodus 28:4, where it is called *mitzneft* and

refers to a part of the High Priest's wardrobe. Another biblical reference is II Samuel 15:30, where covering the head and face is a sign of mourning.
[3]

[3] Sources: "The Jewish Book of Why" by Alfred J. Koltach. Jonathan David Publishers, Inc. New York, 1981.

VII. Tefillin[4]

Tefillin (also called phylacteries) are two small leather boxes that contain verses from the Torah. They are worn on the head and on one arm and are held in place by leather straps. Observant men and boys who have had their Bar Mitzvah usually wear tefillin during the morning prayer services. Women do not usually wear tefillin, though this practice is changing.

Why Do Some Jews Wear Tefillin?
Wearing tefillin is based upon biblical law. Deuteronomy 6:5-9 states:

"Love the Lord your God with all your heart, all your being, and all your might. These words that I am commanding you today must always be on your minds. Recite them to your children. Talk about them when you are sitting around your house and when you are out and about, when you are lying down and when you are getting up. *Tie them on your hand as a sign. They should be on your forehead as a symbol.* Write them on your house's doorframes and on your city's gates."

Though many have interpreted the language of this passage as a figurative reminder to always think about God, the ancient rabbis declared that these words should be taken literally.

---

[4] By Ariela Pelaia

Therefore "Tie them on your hand as a sign" and "They should be on your forehead as a symbol" developed into the leather boxes (tefillin) worn on an individual's arm and head.

In addition to the tefillin themselves, over time customs for how to make tefillin also evolved. Kosher tefillin must be made according to an intricate set of rules that are beyond the scope of this article.

How to Wear Tefillin
Tefillin have two leather boxes, one of which is worn on the arm and the other of which is worn on the head.

If you are right-handed you should wear tefillin on the bicep of your left arm. If you are left-handed, you should wear your tefillin on the bicep of your right arm. In either case, the leather strap holding the box in place should be wrapped around the arm seven times and then six times around the fingers. There is a specific pattern to this wrapping that you should ask your rabbi or a synagogue member who wears tefillin to show you. The tefillin box worn on the head should be centered just above the forehead with the two leather straps wrapping around the head, then hanging down over the shoulders.

Passages Inside the Tefillin
The tefillin boxes contain verses from the Torah. Each verse is handwritten by a scribe with special ink that is used only for parchment scrolls. These passages mention the commandment to wear tefillin and are Deuteronomy 6:4-8, Deuteronomy 11:13-21, Exodus 13:1-10 and Exodus 13:11-16. Excerpts from each of these passages are quoted below.
1. Deuteronomy 6:4-8: "Hear O Israel, the Lord is our God, the Lord is One! You shall love the Lord your God with all your heart, with all your soul and with all your might…These words that I am commanding you today must always be on your minds…Tie them on your hand as a sign. They should be on your forehead as a symbol."
2. Deuteronomy 11:13-21: "If you completely obey God's commandments…by loving the Lord your God and by serving him with

all your heart and all your being, then God will provide rain for your land at the right time… But watch yourselves! Otherwise, your heart might be led astray…Place these words…on your heart and in your very being. Tie them on your hand as a sign. They should be on your forehead as a symbol."

3. Exodus 13:1-10: "The Lord said to Moses: Dedicate to me all your oldest children. Each first offspring from any Israelite womb belongs to me, whether human or animal…Moses said to the people, 'Remember this day which is the day that you came out of Egypt, out of the place you were slaves, because the Lord acted with power to bring you out of there'…You should explain to your child…, 'It's because of what the Lord did for me when I came out of Egypt.' It will be a sign on your hand and a reminder on your forehead so that you will often discuss the Lord's instruction, for the Lord brought you out of Egypt with great power."

4. Exodus 13:11-16: "When the Lord brings you into the land of the Canaanites and gives it to you as promised to you and your ancestors, you should set aside for the Lord whatever comes out of the womb first. All of the first males born to your animal belong to the Lord…When in the future your child asks you, 'What does this mean?' you should answer, 'The Lord brought us with great power out of Egypt, out of the place we were slaves. When Pharaoh refused to let us go, the Lord killed all the oldest offspring in the land of Egypt, from the oldest sons to the oldest male animals. That is why I offer to the Lord as a sacrifice every male that first comes out of the womb. But I ransom my oldest sons.' It will be a sign on your hand and a symbol on your forehead that the lord brought us out of Egypt with great power." (Note: ransoming the oldest son is a ritual known as Pidyon HaBen.)

VIII. Shofar[5]

The *shofar* (שופר) is a Jewish instrument most often made from a ram's horn, though it can also be made from the horn of a sheep or goat. It makes a trumpet-like sound and is traditionally blown on Rosh HaShanah, the Jewish New Year.

Origins of the Shofar

According to some scholars, the *shofar* dates back to ancient times when making loud noises on the New Year was thought to scare off demons and ensure a happy start to the coming year. It is hard to say whether this practice influenced Judaism.

In terms of its Jewish history, the *shofar* is often mentioned in the Tanakh (the Torah, Nevi'im, and Ketuvim, or Torah, Prophets, and Writings), Talmud, and in rabbinic literature. It was used to announce the start of holidays, in processions, and even to mark the start of a war. Perhaps the most famous biblical reference to the *shofar* occurs in the Book of Joshua, where *shofarot* (plural of *shofar*) were used as part of a battle plan to capture the city of Jericho:

---

[5] By Ariela Pelaia

IX. Tallit/Prayer Shawl/TzitTzit[6]

"Speak to the children of Israeland say to them: They shall make for themselves fringes on the corners of their garments… And this shall be tzitzit *for you, and when you see it, you will remember all the commandments of G-d, and perform them" (*Numbers 15:38*-39).*

Most people don't think of Judaism as a fringe religion. Yet that's our uniform and badge of honor, our everyday reminder of who we are and what we're here for—four tassels hanging from the fringes of our clothes.

In ancient times, we would hang the tassels from the fringes of the four-cornered cloaks that were part of people's everyday wardrobe. Today, Jewish men and boys have two ways to do this mitzvah every day:

a) During prayer, wrap yourself in a *tallit gadol* (literally: big cloak). This is the large sheet-like fringed prayer shawl worn during the morning prayers.

b) Wear a little poncho called a *tallit katan* (literally: small cloak). For most of us, it fits neatly under the shirt.

The fringe tassels themselves are called *tzitzit*. Their strings and knots are a physical representation of the Torah's 613 do's and don'ts. It works like this: Each letter in the Hebrew alphabet has a corresponding numerical value. The numerical values of the five letters that comprise the Hebrew word *tzitzit* add up to 600. Add the eight strings and five knots of each tassel, and the total is 613.

Wearing *tzitzit* is a sign of Jewish pride. Jews have always had a way of dress to distinguish them from the people of the lands in which they lived—even when that meant exposing themselves to danger and bigotry. By the grace of G-d, today most of us live in lands where we are free to practice our religion without such fears. Today we wear our Jewish uniform with pride and with our head's held high.

Kabbalah teaches that the *tallit* garment is a metaphor for G-d's infinite transcendent light. The fringes allude to the immanent divine light which permeates every element of creation. By wearing a *tallit gadol* or a *tallit katan*, a Jew synthesizes these two elements and makes them real in his life.

X.   Rosh Chodesh

Rosh Chodesh (sometimes transliterated "Rosh Hodesh") is the Hebrew term for the beginning of a new month on the Jewish calendar. It literally means "head of the month" just as "Rosh HaShanah" (the Jewish New Year) means "head of the year."

The first day of every Hebrew month is called "Rosh Chodesh" and is marked by the appearance of the new moon. The Hebrew calendar follows the cycle of the moon and is therefore a lunar calendar.

Historical Origins of Rosh Chodesh

In ancient Israel the beginning of each month was determined by the testimony of witnesses who had seen the new moon. Witnesses would report their sightings to the Sanhedrin in Jerusalem where they would be asked a series of questions about what they had seen and be presented with a chart of the moon's phases. Once it was determined that two independent witnesses had seen the new moon the Sanhedrin would announce the beginning a Rosh Chodesh using messengers and signal fires to communicate with neighboring communities.

At this time in history Rosh Chodesh was an important event celebrated by family festivities, the blowing of the shofar and sacrifices at the Holy Temple. However, after the destruction of the Second Temple in 70 C.E. the significance of Rosh Chodesh slowly diminished since sacrifices could no longer be offered. Eventually a standardized calendar based upon mathematical knowledge of the lunar cycle was established during the fourth century. This too reduced the significance of Rosh Chodesh.

Rosh Chodesh in the Hebrew Bible (Tanach)

Rosh Chodesh is referenced in the Tanach, which includes the <u>Five Books of Moses</u> (Torah) as well as the Nevi'im (Prophets) and Ketuvim (Writings). In Exodus 12:1-2 God establishes the beginning of the Hebrew calendar, while in Numbers 10:10 God describes the celebration of the new moon:

"Also at your times of rejoicing—your appointed festivals and New Moon feasts —you are to sound the trumpets over your burnt offerings and fellowship offerings, and they will be a memorial for you before your God. I am the Lord your God."

Rosh Chodesh is also referenced in Numbers 28:11 and Psalm 81:3, where the text reads: "Sound the ram's horn at the New Moon, and when the moon is full, on the day of our festival."

Rosh Chodesh in Modern Times

Though Rosh Chodesh is no longer celebrated as a festival holiday, it is nevertheless remembered on Shabbat Mevarechim, which means "the Shabbat that blesses the month." This is the Shabbat directly before Rosh Chodesh and on this day a special prayer is recited that blesses the new month.

At this time the date of Rosh Chodesh and the name of the upcoming Hebrew month are also announced to the congregation.

Shabbat Mevarechim is not observed during the month of Elul because the following month is Tishrei. Since Rosh HaShanah, the Jewish New Year, takes place during Tishrei it is believed that Jews do not need a reminder of when Tishrei begins. (<u>Rosh HaShanah</u> is one of the most important Jewish holidays and therefore the assumption is that most Jews anticipate its coming.)

Rosh Chodesh and Women

Rosh Chodesh has traditionally been associated with women for two reasons: First, according to the <u>midrashic</u> work Pirkei de-Rabbi Eliezer, Rosh Chodesh was given to women as a reward for withholding their jewelry when the Israelites made the Golden Calf during their wanderings in the desert (Exodus 32). In a manner similar to Shabbat, women were given Rosh Chodesh as a day of rest when they were not required to work. The second reason women have often been associated with Rosh Chodesh has to do with similarities between the menstrual cycle and the monthly cycle of the moon.

In addition to these connections, in the Kabbalistic tradition the Shekhinah (the feminine aspect of God) is often compared to the moon. As a result, women are also associated with the moon and therefore Rosh Chodesh.

In modern times some women participate in Rosh Chodesh groups. These groups meet every month, often on the date of Rosh Chodesh for that month, and are composed entirely of women. The customs of each Rosh Chodesh group are determined by its members and their goals for the group. Some groups use this time together to study <u>Torah</u> and other Jewish texts, while other groups may choose to spend their time catching up with friends while enjoying a festive meal, baked goods or tea. Some groups may incorporate study, food and relationship building all in one evening.[7]

---

[7] Telushkin, Joseph. "Jewish Literacy: The Most Important Things to Know About the Jewish Religion, Its People, and Its History. " William Morrow: New York, 1991.

XI. Passover/Unleavened Bread

WHAT IS PASSOVER AND HOW IS IT CELEBRATED?

Passover is both the most-celebrated Jewish holiday of the year and the holiday voted most likely to elicit a groan. People groan when they consider Passover's dietary requirements. They groan when they think of all the preparations. They even groan when they remember how much they overate during Passover last year.

But the real irony behind the moaning, groaning, and *kvetching* is that in some ways this is exactly what you're supposed to feel at this time of year. Passover is a celebration of spring, of birth and rebirth, of a journey from slavery to freedom, and of taking responsibility for yourself, the community, and the world. However, strangely enough, none of this taking of responsibility gets done without groaning. It was with groaning that the Hebrews expressed the pain of their ancient enslavement in Egypt more than 3,300 years ago. It was with groaning that they called attention to their plight. So groan, already!

The Torah states that Jews are to observe Passover for seven days, beginning on the 15th of the Jewish month Nisan (usually in April). The first night always includes a special *seder* (ritual dinner). Plus, traditional Jews outside of Israel don't work on either the first two or the last two days of the seven-day period. Outside of Israel, Jews celebrate a second seder on the second night of Passover.

You can think of Passover as honoring the renewal of the sun (it's always on the first full moon after the Vernal Equinox), or a time to step firmly into springtime. You can also think of Passover as celebrating the Jewish people's "birth certificate" and "Declaration of Independence." Or you can think of it as memorializing something that God did for the Jews 3,300 years ago.

However, to make any celebration or ritual truly meaningful, you must find a way to make it personal. Even Moses — and later the rabbis of the Talmud — recognized this when they instructed the Jewish people how to celebrate Passover. The key isn't only to tell the story of the Exodus, or even to compare your life to the story of the Exodus, but to actually personalize the history: feel the feelings and experience the sensations of this journey. In this way, the Jewish people as individuals and as a people move forward. Everything a person does during Passover aids this process.

Jewish people have four Hebrew names for Passover, each pointing to a particular aspect of the holiday. The most common Hebrew name is *Pesach*, which is usually translated as "passing over," as the Angel of Death passed over the homes of the Jews in Egypt. (Killing the Egyptian first-born was the tenth plague, and it convinced the Pharaoh to release the Hebrews from slavery.) But there are three more Hebrew names for Passover: *Chag Ha-matzot* ("Festival of Unleavened Breads"), *Z'man Cheiruteinu* ("The Time of Liberation"), and *Chag Ha-aviv* ("Festival of Spring").

XII. Shavuot[8]

Shavuot is a Jewish holiday that celebrates the giving of the <u>Torah</u> to the Jews. The Talmud tells us that God gave the Ten Commandments to the Jews on the sixth night of the Hebrew month of Sivan. *Shavuot* always falls 50 days after the second night of Passover. The 49 days in between are known as the <u>Omer</u>.

Origins of Shavuot

In biblical times *Shavuot* also marked the beginning of the new agricultural season and was called *Hag HaKatzir*, which means "The Harvest Holiday." Other names *Shavuot* is known by are "The Feast of Weeks" and *Hag HaBikurim*, meaning "The Holiday of First Fruits." This last name comes from the practice of bringing fruits to the Temple on *Shavuot*.

After the destruction of the Temple in 70 CE the rabbis connected *Shavuot* with the Revelation at Mt. Sinai, when God gave the Ten Commandments to the Jewish people. This is why *Shavuot* celebrates the giving and receiving of the Torah in modern times.

Celebrating Shavuot Today

Many religious Jews commemorate *Shavuot* by spending the entire night studying Torah at their synagogue or at home.
They also study other biblical books and portions of the Talmud. This all-night gathering is known as *Tikun Leyl Shavuot* and at dawn participants stop studying and recite *shacharit*, the morning prayer.

---

[8] By Ariela Pelaia

Tikun Leyl Shavuot is a *kabbalistic* (mystical) custom that is relatively new to Jewish tradition. It is increasingly popular among modern Jews and is meant to help us rededicate ourselves to studying Torah. Kabbalists taught that at midnight on *Shavuot* the skies open for a brief moment and God favorably hears all prayers.

In addition to study, other *Shavuot* customs include:

Chanting the Ten Commandments.

Reading *Megilat Rut*, known as the Book of Ruth in English. This biblical book tells the story of two women: a Jewish woman named Naomi and her non-Jewish daughter-in-law Ruth. Their relationship was so strong that when Ruth's husband died she decided to join the Jewish people by converting to Judaism. The Book of Ruth is read during *Shavuot* because it takes place during the harvest season and because Ruth's conversion is thought to reflect our acceptance of the Torah on *Shavuot*. Also, Jewish tradition teaches that King David (Ruth's great-great-grandson) was born and died on *Shavuot*.

Decorating our synagogues and homes with roses or aromatic spices. This custom is based on *midrashim* that connect the events at Sinai to spices and roses.

The Foods of Shavuot

Jewish holidays often have some food-related component and *Shavuot* is no different. According to tradition we should eat dairy foods such as cheese, cheesecake and milk on *Shavuot*. No one knows where this custom comes from but some think it is related to *Shir HaShirim* (The Song of Songs). One line of this poem reads "Honey and milk are under your tongue." Many believe that this line is comparing the Torah to the sweetness of milk and honey. In some European cities children are introduced to Torah study on *Shavuot* and are given honey cakes with passages from the Torah written on them.

XIII. Yom Teruah/Rosh HaShanah[9]

Rosh Hashanah

What: It is the birthday of the universe, the day G-d created Adam and Eve, and it's celebrated as the head of the Jewish year.
When: The first two days of the Jewish year, Tishrei 1 and 2, beginning at sundown on the eve of Tishrei
How: Candle lighting in the evenings, festive meals with sweet delicacies during the night and day, prayer services that include the sounding of the ram's horn *(shofar)* on both mornings, and desisting from creative work.

Why Rosh Hashanah Is Important

Rosh Hashanah means "Head of the Year." Just like the head controls the body, our actions on Rosh Hashanah have a tremendous impact on the rest of the year.

As we read in the Rosh Hashanah prayers, each year on this day "all inhabitants of the world pass before G-d like a flock of sheep," and it is decreed in the heavenly court "who shall live, and who shall die ... who shall be impoverished and who shall be enriched; who shall fall and who shall rise."

It is a day of prayer, a time to ask the Almighty to grant us a year of peace, prosperity and blessing. But it is also a joyous day when we proclaim G-d King of the Universe. The Kabbalists teach that the continued existence of the universe depends on G-d's desire for a world, a desire that is renewed when we accept His kingship anew each year on Rosh Hashanah.

What's It Called?
• The most common name for this holiday is Rosh Hashanah, the name used in the eponymous tractate of Talmud devoted to the holiday.
• The Torah refers to this day as Yom Teruah (Day of Shofar Blowing).[1]
• In our prayers, we often call it Yom Hazikaron (Day of Remembrance) and Yom Hadin (Day of Judgement) since this is the day when G-d recalls all of His creations and determines their fate for the year ahead.

First Priority: Hear the Shofar

The central observance of Rosh Hashanah is the sounding of the _shofar,_ the ram's horn, on both mornings of the holiday (except if the first day is Shabbat, in which case we blow the _shofar_ only on the second day).
The first 30 blasts of the _shofar_ are blown following the Torah reading during morning services, and as many as 70 are then blown during (and immediately after) the Musaf service. Many communities listen to 100 blastsover the course of the Rosh Hashanah morning services. For someone who cannot come to synagogue, the _shofar_ may be blown the rest of the day. If you cannot make it out, please contact your closest Chabad center to see about arranging a "house call."
The _shofar_ blowing contains a series of three types of blasts: _tekiah_, a long sob-like blast; _shevarim_, a series of three short wails; and _teruah_, at least nine piercing staccato bursts.
(Read more about the _shofar_ blasts, here.)
The blowing of the _shofar_ represents the trumpet blast that is sounded at a king's coronation. Its plaintive cry also serves as a call to repentance.
The _shofar_ itself recalls the Binding of Isaac, an event that occurred on Rosh Hashanah in which a ram took Isaac's place as an offering to G-d. (Read more on the reasons for shofar here.)

Other Rosh Hashanah Observances

Greetings: When you meet a fellow Jew on the first night of Rosh Hashanah, wish him, *"Leshana tovah tikatev v'tichatem"* or, for a female,*"Leshana tovah tikatevee v'tichatemee"* ("May you be inscribed and sealed for a good year"). Afterward, wish them a *"G'mar chatimah tovah"* ("A good inscription and sealing [in the Book of Life]"). (More on the Rosh Hashanah greetings here.)

Candles: As with every major Jewish holiday, women and girls light candles on each evening of Rosh Hashanah and recite the appropriate blessings. On the second night, make sure to use an existing flame and think about a new fruit that you will be eating (or garment that you are wearing) while you say the Shehechiyanu blessing. Click here for candle lighting times in your area and here for the blessings.

Tashlich: On the first afternoon of Rosh Hashanah (provided that it is notShabbat), it is customary to go to a body of water (ocean, river, pond, etc.) and perform the Tashlich ceremony, in which we ceremonially cast our sins into the water. With this tradition we are symbolically evoking the verse, "And You shall cast their sins into the depths of the sea." The short prayer for this service can be found in your *machzor*.

Rosh Hashanah Prayers

Much of the day is spent in synagogue. The evening and afternoon prayers are similar to the prayers said on a regular holiday. However, the morning services are significantly longer.

The holiday prayerbook—called a *machzor*—contains all the prayers and Torah readings for the entire day. The most significant addition is the *shofar* blowing ceremony. However, there are also other important elements of the prayer service that are unique to Rosh Hashanah. The Torah is read on both mornings of Rosh Hashanah. On the first day, we read about Isaac's birth and the subsequent banishment of Hagar and Ishmael.[2] Appropriately, the reading is followed by a *haftarah* reading about the birth of Samuel the Prophet.[3] Both readings contain the theme of prayers for children being answered, and both of these births took place on Rosh Hashanah.

On the second morning, we read about Abraham's near-sacrifice of his son Isaac.[4] As mentioned above, the *shofar* blowing recalls the ram, which figures prominently in this story as a powerful display of Abraham's devotion to G-d that has characterized His children ever since. The *haftarah*[5] tells of G-d's eternal love for His people.

The cantor's repetition of the Amidah (Silent Prayer) is peppered with *piyyutim,* poetic prayers that express our prayerful wishes for the year and other themes of the day. For certain selections, those deemed especially powerful, the ark is opened. Many of these additions are meant to be said responsively, as a joint effort between the prayer leader and the congregation.

Even without the added *piyyutim,* the Rosh Hashanah Musaf prayer is significantly longer than it is the rest of the year. This is because its single middle blessing is divided into three additional blessings, each focusing on another one of the holiday's main themes: G-d's kingship, our wish that He "remember" us for the good, and the *shofar.* Each blessing contains a collage of Biblical verses that express its theme, and is then followed by a round of *shofar* blowing.

Rosh Hashanah Feasts

We eat festive meals every night and day of the holiday. Like all other holiday meals, we begin by reciting <u>kiddush</u> over wine and then say the blessing over bread. But there are some important differences:
a. The bread (traditionally baked into <u>round</u> challah loaves, and often sprinkled with raisins) is dipped into honey instead of salt, expressing our wish for a sweet year. We do this on Rosh Hashanah, Shabbat Shuvah (the Shabbat before Yom Kippur), in the pre-Yom Kippur meal and during Sukkot.

b. Furthering the sweet theme, it is traditional to begin the meal on the first night with slices of apple dipped in honey. Before eating the apple, we make the *ha'eitz* blessing and then say, "May it be Your will to renew for us a good and sweet year."

c. Many people eat parts of the head of a fish or a ram, expressing the wish that "we be a head and not a tail."

d. In many communities, there are additional traditional foods eaten, each symbolizing a wish for the coming year. Many eat pomegranates, giving voice to a wish that "our merits be many like the [seeds of the] pomegranate." Another common food is *tzimmes,* a sweet carrot-based dish eaten because of its Yiddish name, *merren*, which means both "carrot" and "increase," symbolizing a wish for a year of abundance.

e. It is traditional to avoid nuts (here's why) as well as vinegar-based, sharp foods, most notably the horseradish traditionally eaten with gefilte fish, since we don't want a bitter year.

f. On the second night of the holiday, we do not eat the apples, fish heads, pomegranates, etc. However, before we break bread (and dip it in honey), we eat a "new fruit," something we have not tasted since the last time it was in season. (Read this blog post to learn the reason for the new fruit and the other traditional foods.)

XIV. Yom Kippur[10]

Yom Kippur (the Day of Atonement) is one of two Jewish High Holy Days. The first High Holy Day is Rosh Hashanah (the Jewish New Year). Yom Kippur falls ten days after Rosh Hashanah on the 10th of Tishrei, which is a Hebrew month that correlates with September-October on the secular calendar. The purpose of Yom Kippur is to bring about reconciliation between people and between individuals and God. According to Jewish tradition, it is also the day when God decides the fate of each human being.

Although Yom Kippur is an intense holiday it is nevertheless viewed as a happy day. Why? Because if one has observed the holiday properly by the end of Yom Kippur they will have made peace with others and with God.

There are three essential components of Yom Kippur:

- <u>Teshuvah</u> (Repentance)
- Prayer
- Fasting

Teshuvah (Repentance)

Yom Kippur is a Day of Reconciliation, when Jews strive to make amends with people and to draw closer to God through prayer and fasting.

The ten days leading up to Yom Kippur are known as the Ten Days of Repentance. During this period Jews are encouraged to seek out anyone they may have offended and to sincerely request forgiveness so that the

---

[10] By Ariela Pelaia

New Year can begin with a clean slate. If the first request for forgiveness is rebuffed, one should ask for forgiveness at least two more times, at which point the person whose forgiveness is being sought should grant the request. The rabbis thought it was cruel for anyone to withhold their forgiveness for offenses that had not caused irrevocable damage. Learn more about teshuvah.

This process of repentance is called *teshuvah* and it is a crucial part of Yom Kippur. Although many people think that transgressions from the previous year are forgiven through prayer, fasting and participation in Yom Kippur services, Jewish tradition teaches that only offenses committed against God can be forgiven on Yom Kippur. Hence it is important that people make an effort to reconcile with others before participating in Yom Kippur services.

Prayer

Yom Kippur is the longest synagogue service in the Jewish year. It begins on the evening before Yom Kippur day with a haunting song called Kol Nidre (All Vows). The words of this melody ask God to forgive any vows people have made to God and not kept.

The service on the day of Yom Kippur lasts from morning until nightfall. Many prayers are said but one is repeated at intervals throughout the service. This prayer is called Al Khet and asks for forgiveness for a variety of sins that may have been committed during the year. The Jewish concept of sin is not like the Christian concept of original sin. Rather, it's the kind of everyday offenses like hurting those we love, lying to ourselves or using foul language that Judaism views as sinful. You can clearly see examples of these infractions in the Yom Kippur liturgy, for instance in this excerpt from Al Khet:

For the sin that we have committed under stress or through choice;
For the sin that we have committed in stubbornness or in error;
For the sin that we have committed in the evil meditations of the heart;
For the sin that we have committed by word of mouth;

For the sin that we have committed through abuse of power;
For the sin that we have committed by exploitation of neighbors;
For all these sins, O God of forgiveness, bear with us, pardon us, forgive us!

When Al Khet is recited people gently beat their fists against their chests as each sin is mentioned. Sins are mentioned in plural form because even if someone hasn't committed a particular sin, Jewish tradition teaches that every Jew bears a measure of responsibility for the actions of other Jews.

During the afternoon portion of the Yom Kippur service the Book of Jonah is read to remind people of God's willingness to forgive those who are sincerely sorry. The last part of the service is called Ne'ilah (Shutting). The name comes from the imagery of Ne'ilah prayers, which talk about gates being shut against us. People pray intensely during this time, hoping to be admitted to God's presence before the gates have been shut.

Fasting

Yom Kippur is also marked by 25 hours of fasting. There are other fast days in the Jewish calendar, but this is the only one the Torah specifically commands us to observe. Leviticus 23:27 describes it as "afflicting your souls" and during this time no food or liquid may be consumed.

The fast starts an hour before Yom Kippur begins and ends after nightfall on the day of Yom Kippur. In addition to food, Jews are also forbidden from engaging in sexual relations, bathing or wearing leather shoes. The prohibition against wearing leather comes from a reluctance to wear the skin of a slaughtered animal while asking God for mercy.

Who Fasts on Yom Kippur

Children under the age of nine are not allowed to fast, while children older than nine are encouraged to eat less. Girls who are 12 years or older and boys who are 13 years or older are required to participate in the full

25-hour fast along with adults. However, pregnant women, women who have recently given birth and anyone suffering from a life-threatening illness are not required to observe the fast. These people need food and drink to keep up their strength and Judaism always values life above the observance of Jewish law.

Many people end the fast with a feeling of deep serenity, which comes from having made peace with others and with God. If you would like to learn more about fasting, check out this About.com article:

XV. Sukkot

Sukkot is an seven-day harvest holiday that arrives during the Hebrew month of Tishrei. It starts four days after <u>Yom Kippur</u> and is followed by <u>Shmini Atzeret</u> and <u>Simchat Torah</u>. Sukkot is also known as the Festival of Booths and the Feast of Tabernacles.

The Origin of Sukkot

Sukkot hearkens back to times in ancient Israel when Jews would build huts near the edges of their fields during the harvest season. One of these dwellings was called a "sukkah" and "sukkot" is the plural form of this Hebrew word. These dwellings not only provided shade but allowed the workers to maximize the amount of time they spent in the fields, harvesting their food more quickly as a result.

Sukkot is also related to the way the Jewish people lived while wandering in the desert for 40 years (Leviticus 23:42-43). As they moved from one place to another they built tents or booths, called sukkot, that gave them temporary shelter in the desert.

Hence, the sukkot (booths) that Jews build during the holiday of Sukkot are reminders both of Israel's agricultural history and of the Israelite exodus from Egypt.

Traditions of Sukkot

There are three major traditions associated with Sukkot:

Eating in the sukkah.

Waving the lulav and etrog.

At the <u>beginning</u> of sukkot (often during the days between Yom Kippur and Sukkot) Jews construct a sukkah. In ancient times people would live in the sukkot and eat every meal in them. In modern times people most often build a sukkah in their backyards or help their synagogue construct one for the community.

Few people live in the sukkah today but it is popular to eat at least one meal in it. At the beginning of the meal a special blessing is recited, which goes: "Blessed are you, Adonai our God, Ruler of the universe, who has sanctified us with commandments, and commanded us to dwell in the sukkah." If it is raining then the commandment to eat in the sukkah is postponed until the weather is more accommodating.

Since Sukkot celebrates the harvest in the land of Israel, <u>another custom on Sukkot</u> involves waving the lulav and etrog. Together the lulav and etrog represent the <u>Four Species</u>. The etrog is a kind of citron (related to a lemon), while the lulav is made of three myrtle twigs (hadassim), two willow twigs (aravot) and a palm frond (lulav). Because the palm frond is the largest of these plants, the myrtle and willow are wrapped around it. During Sukkot, the lulav and etrog are waved together while reciting special blessings. They are waved in each of the four directions - sometimes six if "up" and "down" are included in the ritual - representing God's dominion over Creation.

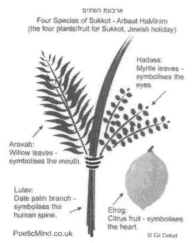

אַרְבַּעַת הַמִּינִים
Four Species of Sukkot - Arbaat HaMinim
(the four plants/fruit for Sukkot, Jewish holiday)

Hadass:
Myrtle leaves -
symbolises the
eyes.

Aravah:
Willow leaves -
symbolises the mouth.

Lulav:
Date palm branch -
symbolises the
human spine.

Etrog:
Citrus fruit - symbolises
the heart.

PoeticMind.co.uk

© Gil Dekel

The lulav and etrog are also part of the synagogue service. On each morning of Sukkot people will carry the lulav and etrog around the sanctuary while reciting prayers. On the seventh day of Sukkot, called Hoshana Rabba, the Torah is removed from the Ark and congregants march around the synagogue seven times while holding the lulav and etrog.

The eighth and last day of Sukkot is known as Shmeni Atzeret. On this day a prayer for rain is recited, demonstrating how the Jewish holidays are in tune with the seasons of Israel, which begins on this day.

The Quest for the Perfect Etrog

Among religious circles a unique aspect of Sukkot involves the quest for the perfect etrog. Some people will spend upwards of $100 for the perfect etrog .

XVI. Prayer Siddur[11]

In Judaism, the *siddur* is the ultimate prayer book that guides Jews through the multitude of daily prayers, whether a regular day or a special holiday or festival.

Meaning

The word *siddur* (סדור; plural, *siddurim*) comes from the word seder, which means "order." The *siddur* is, essentially, the order of prayer and is a book that contains the three daily prayers:

- morning, or *shacharit*
- afternoon, or *mincha*
- evening, or *ma'ariv*

There's also countless other prayers contained in a regular *siddur*, including the blessings after eating, the mourner's blessings, prayers for visiting different holy locations, and more. The collection of prayers and blessings varies from *siddur* to *siddur*, and there are even those that simply contain the daily set prayers or those specifically for Shabbat and nothing more.

Origins

The origins of the *siddur* as set daily prayers might seem odd, considering this note from Rabbi Eliezer in Mishnah Brachot 4:4:

---

[11] By Chaviva Gordon-Bennett

"One who makes one's prayers fixed, that person's prayers are not sincere petitions."

Despite this, an order and process were necessary for the Jewish people to carry on after the destruction of the Temple in 70 CE (Common Era). The service, or order, of Jewish prayer was established large in part during the first four or five centuries of the common era during the Talmudic period.

The oldest *siddur* in the world dates to the 9th century during a time when the official "canon" was more or less finalized by the Babylonian *geonim*, who were the great and leading Jewish leaders of the 6th-11th centuries.

The Service

- As the most complex of the three daily services, the morning service, or *shacharit*, has two primary parts:
- **The Shema:** This is three paragraphs from *Devarim* (Deuteronomy) 6 and 11 and *BaMidbar* (Numbers) 15 that are core to the basic beliefs of Judaism.
- **The Amidah:** The core of every prayer service, this is a set of seven blessings on Shabbat or 19 blessings on a weekday that highlight repentance. There are additional blessings on holidays and services for a new Hebrew month.
- There are many other prayers, verses, and blessings throughout the services, including the *P'sukei d'Zimrah* (Psalms and songs of blessings, among others) and Hallel (a series of Psalms).
- Over time, various prayers were added as the centuries changed and evolved and poetic renditions of prayers, like *Adon Olam* (Eternal Lord) and *Yigdal* (which is an adaption of the Rambam's "Thirteen Principles of Faith") in the Middle Ages were added to the prayer book.

Different Customs, Different *Siddurim*

There are countless versions of the *siddur* in the Jewish world, and each version not only varies by the types of prayers and blessings it contains but also customs and denominations.

In Orthodox Judaism, a *nusach*, which is a Hebrew term meaning "text" or "form," is related to customs or traditions of a specific practice of prayer. For example, Jews from Yemen have a specific *nusach* or *minhag* (מנהג) in which they pray, just as Ashkenazi Jews do. This means that there are different additions and exemptions, orders and styles of prayer services for different communities. Some examples of the different *nusachs*:

- **Nusach Sfard:** Despite its name, this is actually a *siddur* that is used almost universally by Hasidim use and very few Sephardim use. The *siddur* reconciles Ashkenazi customs with those of the great mystic and Rabbi Isaac Luria (the Ari).
- **Nusach Ashkenaz:** As its name suggests, this is a *siddur* with the customs of Eastern and Central European Jews. There is also Nusach Polin, but this is usually only used in reference to the *selichot* service of penitential prayers and not the entire prayer service.
- **Nusach Ari** (or Chabad): Although a Hasidic sect, Chabad Jews use a specific *sitter* that is based on the teachings of the mystic and Rabbi Isaac Luria (the Ari), mentioned above, but with enough differences that it is uniquely different than Nusach Sfard.
- **Nusach Sephardi and Mizrachi:** There are countless variations of this *nusach*, with the customs of communities in Spain, Italy, Morocco, Syria, Salonica (Greece), and so on.
- Nuscah Teman: The Jews of Yemenite have their own unique *nusach* and thus, *siddur*, that has the unique Temani pronunciation of the Hebrew cantillation (the marks that tell one how to recite the Torah and prayer service) that is believed to most closely match the Hebrew of Ancient Israel.

- **Nusach Eretz Yisrael:** The is among the most modern *nusachim,* and is used in mostly in Machon Shilo, a center of Jewish learning in Jerusalem. It is gaining ground across Israel because it has prayers that are unique to the land of Israel itself, creating an easy-to-use *nusach* for when you're in Israel.
- There are countless other *nusachs* and each Jew is encouraged to choose the tradition or custom of prayer that fits their own individual prayer style.
- There are also unique prayer books to the different movements, whether Conservative, Masorti, Reform, Renewal, or Reconstructionist Judaism. In addition to different *siddurim* for different movements, there are also prayerbooks within each movement that have translations and transliterations. Some prayer books have Hebrew on the left side of the page with English translations on the right (this is common with the Orthodox movement's Koren *siddurim*) and others have Hebrew on the right and English on the left (this is common with Orthodox movement's Artscroll *siddurim*).

Commentary

Oftentimes, *siddurim* will be filled with various commentary as a point of education and information for the user. As the prayer book is one of the most ubiquitous of Jewish texts, found in every Jewish home, synagogue, Jewish school, and, in Israel, in gas stations and convenience stores alike, it's a great place for thoughts and explanations for the prayer service. Depending on what *nusach* you're using, there will be commentaries from great medieval rabbis, Hasidic thought, and modern understandings of unique additions to the prayer service (e.g., prayers for local government, the State of Israel, the Israel Defense Forces soldiers).

Personal Prayer

Although there is a structured *siddur* that every Jew follows in daily prayers, individual and personal prayer is still an incredibly huge part of the Jewish experience. In fact, *hitbodedut* (התבודדות), is a type of self-seclusion prayer that was championed by Rebbe Nachman of Breslov, who believed that no topic was too mundane to discuss with God. In Sichos HaRan #7, Rebbe Nachman says,

It is very good to pour out your thoughts before God, like a child pleading before his father. God calls us His children, as it is written (Deuteronomy 14:1), "You are children to the Lord your God." Therefore, it is good to express your thoughts and troubles to God, like a child complaining and pestering his father.

You may think that you have done so much wrong that you are no longer one of God's children, but remember that God still calls you His child. We are taught, "For good or for evil you are always called his children." Let us assume that God has dismissed you and told you that you are no longer His child. Still you must say, "Let Him do as He wills. I must do my part and still act like His child." How very good it is, when you can awaken your heart and plead until tears stream from your eyes, and you stand like a little child crying before its Father.

XVII.   Shabbat (Challah, Candles, Wine)

Every week, Jews around the world of varying observances take time to rest, reflect, and enjoy on Shabbat. In fact, the Talmud says that to observe the Sabbath is equal to all of the commandments combined! But what is this weekly observance?

Meaning and Origins

Shabbat (שבת) translates to English as Sabbath, meaning to rest or to cease. In Judaism this specifically refers to the period of time from Friday sundown to Saturday sundown in which Jews were commanded to avoid all acts of work and kindling of fire.

The origins for Shabbat come, obviously enough, in the beginning in Genesis 2:1-3:

"The heaven and earth were finished, and all their array. On the seventh day God finished the work (*melacha)* that God had been doing, and God ceased [rested] on the seventh day from all the work which God had done. And God blessed the seventh day and declared it holy, because on it God ceased [rested] from all the work of creation which God had done."
The importance of rest from creation is elevated later in the declaration of the commandments, or *mitzvot*.

"Remember the Sabbath day and keep it holy. Six days you shall labor and do all your work (*melacha*), but the seventh day is a Sabbath of your God: you shall not do any work, you, your son or daughter, your male or female slave, or your cattle, or the stranger who is within your settlements. For in six days, God made heaven and earth and sea, all that is in them, and God rested on the seventh day; therefore God has blessed the Sabbath day and hallowed it" (Exodus 20:8-11).

And in a repetition of the commandments:

"Observe the Sabbath day and keep it holy, as your God has commanded you. Six days you shall labor and do all your work (*melacha*), but the seventh day is a Sabbath of your God: you shall not do any work, you, your son or your daughter, your male or female slave, your ox of your ass, or any of your cattle, or the stranger in your settlements, so that your male and female slave may rest as you do. Remember that you were a slave in the land of Egypt and your God freed you from there with a mighty hand and an outstretched arm; therefore your God has commanded you to observe the Sabbath day (Deuteronomy 5:12-15).

Later, the promise of a proud heritage is presented in Isaiah 58:13-14 if the Sabbath day is properly observed.

"If you restrain your foot because of Shabbat, from performing your affairs on My holy day, and you call the Sabbath a delight, the holy of the Lord honored, and you honor it by not doing your wonted ways, by not pursuing your affairs and speaking words, then, you shall delight with the Lord, and I will cause you to ride on the high places of the land, and I will give you to eat the heritage of Jacob your father, for the mouth of the Lord has spoken."

Shabbat is a day in which Jews are commanded to *shamor v'zachor* -- to observe and remember. The Sabbath is meant as a day of cessation, to truly appreciate what goes into work and creation. By stopping for 25 hours once every week, it's possible to appreciate so much of what we take for granted throughout the week, whether it is the ease of cooking in a microwave or oven or the ability to hop in the car and run to the grocery store.

The 39 Melachot

Although the most basic commandment from the Torah, or Hebrew Bible, is to not work or kindle a fire, over a period of thousands of years the Sabbath has evolved and developed with the understanding of scholars and sages.

After all, the term "work" or "labor" (Hebrew, *melacha*) is broad and can encompass many different things to many different people (for a baker work is baking and producing food but for a policeman work is defending and enforcing the law). In Genesis the term is used for creation, while in Exodus and Deuteronomy it is used to refer to work or labor. Thus the rabbis evolved what became known as the 39 *melachot*, or forbidden activities, on Shabbat in order to make sure Jews were avoiding all acts of creation, work, or labor so as to not violate the Sabbath.

These 39 *melachot* evolved in regards to the "labor" involved in the creation of the *mishkan,* or tabernacle, that was built while the Israelites sojourned in the wilderness in Exodus and can be found within six categories detailed in *Mishnah Shabbat* 73a. Although they might seem abstract, there are many <u>modern examples for the 39 *melachot*</u>.

- **Field Work**
- Sowing
- Plowing
- Reaping
- Binding Sheaves
- Threshing
- Winnowing
- Selecting
- Grinding
- Sifting
- Kneading
- Baking
- **Making Material Curtains**
- Shearing Wool

- Cleaning
- Combing
- Dyeing
- Spinning
- Stretching the Threads
- Making Loops
- Weaving Threads
- Separating the Threads
- Tying a Knot
- Untying a Knot
- Sewing
- Tearing
- **Making Leather Curtains**
- Trapping
- Slaughtering
- Skinning
- Tanning
- Smoothing
- Ruling Lines
- Cutting
- **Making the Beams for the *Mishkan***
- Writing
- Erasing
- **Building and Breaking Down the *Mishkan***
- Building
- Breaking Down
- **Final Touches**
- Extinguishing a Fire
- Kindling a Fire
- Striking the Final Hammer Blow
- Carrying (from which we derive the need for the *eruv*)

How To

Beyond the 39 *melachot*, there are many components of Shabbat observance, starting with lighting the Shabbat candles on Friday night and ending with another candle-related practice called *havdalah*, which separates the sacred from the profane. (A day in Judaism begins at sundown, rather than sunrise.)

Depending on individual observance, any mix-and-match approach to the following can be undertaken on Shabbat. Here is a quick chronological view of what a typical Friday and Saturday might look like.

- **Friday:**
- During the day Friday, Jews clean their homes and themselves from top to bottom and dress their best and decorate their tables with the cleanest linens in order to welcome the Sabbath bride (*Talmud Shabbat* 119a)
- At sundown, light Shabbat candles with a *bracha* (blessing)
- Evening prayer services (*ma'ariv*) at synagogue
- Before the festive dinner, everyone at the table sings *Shalom Aleichem* and *Aishes Chayil*, followed by the the blessing of the children
- Before the meal, the blessings of *kiddush* over wine and *ha'motzi* over *challah* are recited
- The festive Shabbat meal takes place, sometimes going well into the night with singing and discussions about the weekly Torah portion (known as the *parsha*)

- **Saturday:**
- Morning (*shacharit*) prayer services at synagogue
- A festive lunch preceded by the blessings of *kiddush* over wine and *ha'motzi* over *challah* before the meal
- Afternoon nap or learning at synagogue or home
- Afternoon (*mincha*) prayer services at synagogue

- An informal, yet festive, third meal, called _shalushudis_ or _seudah shlishit_, with _ha'motzi_ over _challah_ before the meal
- Evening prayer services (_ma'ariv_) at synagogue
- _Havdalah_ at the synagogue and/or at home roughly one hour after sundown
- In some cases, on Saturday night after _havdalah_, another festive meal called a _melavah malkah_ takes place to "escort" the Sabbath bride out.

Where to Begin?

If you're just taking on Shabbat for the first time, take small steps and savor each moment of rest by

- going to a Shabbat meal
- turning off your mobile phone and the TV for 25 hours
- don't spend any money for 25 hours
- light Shabbat candles on Friday night
- make _challah_
- go to synagogue
- If you're not sure where to start, find a Messianic Congregation and start learing abouty our Judaic Roots in Messiah Yeshua.

XVIII.   Bar/Bat Mitzvah

Bar Mitzvah literally **translates as "son of commandment." The word "bar" means "son"** in Aramaic, which was the commonly spoken vernacular language of the Jewish people (and much of the Middle East) from around 500 B.C.E. to 400 C.E. The word "mitzvah" is Hebrew for "commandment." The term "bar mitzvah" refers to two things:

- First, when a boy comes of age at 13-years-old he has become a "bar mitzvah" and is recognized by Jewish tradition as having the same rights as a full grown man. A boy who has become a Bar Mitzvah is now morally and ethically responsible for his decisions and actions.
- The term "bar mitzvah" also refers to the religious ceremony that accompanies a boy becoming a Bar Mitzvah. Often a celebratory party will follow the ceremony and that party is also called a bar mitzvah.
- This article is about the religious ceremony and party referred to as a bar mitzvah. For more information about becoming bar mitzvah please read: "What Does It Mean to 'Become Bar Mitzvah?'"
- It is important to note that the ceremony and celebration are not required by Jewish custom. Rather, a Jewish boy automatically becomes Bar Mitzvah at 13-years-old. Although the specifics of the ceremony and party will vary widely depending on which movement (Orthodox, Conservative, Reform, etc.) the family is a member of below are the basics of a Bar Mitzvah.

Bat Mitzvah literally means "daughter of commandment." The word "bat" means "daughter" in Aramaic, which was the commonly spoken language of the Jewish people (and much of the Middle East) from about 500 B.C.E. to 400 C.E. The word "mitzvah" is Hebrew for "commandment."

The term "bat mitzvah" refers to two things:

- When a girl reaches 12-years-old she becomes a "bat mitzvah" and is recognized by Jewish tradition as having the same rights as an adult. She is now morally and ethically responsible for her decisions and actions.
- "Bat Mitzvah" also refers to a religious ceremony that accompanies a girl becoming a Bat Mitzvah. Often a celebratory party will follow the ceremony and that party is also called a bat mitzvah.
- This article is about the religious ceremony and party referred to as a bat mitzvah. The specifics of the ceremony and party (even whether there is a religious ceremony to mark the occasion) vary widely depending on which movement of Judaism (Orthodox, Conservative, Reform, etc.) the family belongs to.

The Ceremony

While a special religious service or ceremony is not required for a boy to become a Bar Mitzvah, over the centuries a greater and greater emphasis has been placed on the ceremony as a right of passage of sorts. The earliest observance marking this point in a boy's life was simply his first *aliyah*, where he would be called up to recite the Torah reading blessings at the first Torah service after his 13th birthday.
In modern practice, the bar mitzvah ceremony usually requires much more preparation and participation on the part of the boy, who will work with a Rabbi and/or Cantor for months (or years) studying for the event. While the exact role he plays in the service will vary between the different

Jewish movements and synagogues it usually involves some or all of the elements below:

- Leading specific prayers or the entire service during a Shabbat service or, less commonly, weekday religious service.
- Reading the weekly Torah portion during a Shabbat service or, less commonly, weekday religious service. Often the boy will learn and use the traditional chant for the reading.

- Reading the weekly Haftarah portion during a Shabbat service or, less commonly, weekday religious service. Often the boy will learn and use the traditional chant for the reading.

- Giving a speech about the Torah and/or Haftarah reading.

- Completing a tzedakah (charity) project leading up to the ceremony to raise money or donations for a charity of the bar mitzvah's choice.
- The family of the Bar Mitzvah is often honored and recognized during the service with an aliyah or multiple aliyahs. It has also become the custom in many synagogues for the Torah to be passed from grandfather to father to the Bar Mitzvah, symbolizing the passing down of the obligation to engage in the study of Torah and Judaism.
- While the bar mitzvah ceremony is a milestone life-cycle event in the life of a Jewish boy and is the culmination of years of study, it is actually not the end of a boy's Jewish education. It simply marks the beginning of a lifetime of Jewish learning, study and participation in the Jewish community.

XIX. Star of David/Flag of Israel[12]

The Star of David

Unlike the menora (candelabrum), the Lion of Judah, the shofar (ram's horn) and the lulav (palm frond), the Star of David was never a uniquely Jewish symbol. The standard name for the geometric shape is a hexagram or six-pointed star, composed of two interlocking equilateral triangles. In a classic article, Gershom Sholem shed light on the history of the "Star of David" and its connection with Judaism and tried to answer the question whether it was appropriate to include it in the national flag or state emblem.*

One of the first Jewish uses of the Star of David was as part of a colophon, the special emblem printed on the title page of a book. Sometimes the printer included his family name in the colophon; or chose an illustration that alluded to his name, ancestry, or the local prince, or a symbol of success and blessing. The idea was to differentiate this printer's books from those of his competitors and to embellish the title page. Colophons are as old as the printing press itself.

According to Sholem, the motive for the widespread use of the Star of David was a wish to imitate Christianity. During the Emancipation, Jews needed a symbol of Judaism parallel to the cross, the universal symbol of Christianity. In particular, they wanted something to adorn the walls of the modern Jewish house of worship that would be symbolic like the cross. This is why the Star of David became prominent in the nineteenth century and why it was later used on ritual objects and in synagogues and eventually reached Poland and Russia. The pursuit of imitation, in

---

[12] Jewish Virtual Library

Sholem's opinion, led to the dissemination of an emblem that was not really Jewish and conveyed no Jewish message. In his opinion, it was also the reason why the Star of David satisfied Zionism: it was a symbol which had already attained wide circulation among the Jewish communities but at the same time evoked no clear-cut religious associations. The Star of David became the emblem of Zionist Jews everywhere. Non-Jews regarded it as representing not only the Zionist current in Judaism, but Jewry as a whole.

The Blue Stripes

The blue stripes on the Zionist flag were inspired by the stripes on the tallit (prayer shawl). The tallit has two separate symbolic aspects: the light blue hue and the stripes. Some say that the stripes are meant to recall the one dyed strand of the ritual fringes (tzitzit). This leads to the significance of the hue itself. According to the Torah, one strand in the tzitzit should be light blue. To judge from references in the Talmud, it was a shade between green and blue. Many symbolic meanings were attributed to it. Rabbi Meir said that it recalls the color of the sky; Rabbi Judah ben Illai maintained that the color of Aaron's staff was light blue, as were the Tablets of the Law, and this is why God commanded the Jews to include it on their prayer shawls: "As long as the people of Israel are looking at this tehelet, they are reminded of {the words} written on the tablets and observe them." In other words, the sight of the color tehelet leads to observance of the commandments. White and tehelet, along with gold and purple, were the colors of the High Priest's raiment (Exodus 28: 4,43) and of the curtains of the Tabernacle (Exodus 26). They were considered to be the colors of purity symbolizing the spirituality of the Jewish people.

Frankl's poem was translated into flowery Hebrew and appeared in the periodical Hahavatzelet (The Rose of Sharon) in 1878. We do not know if the founders of Zionism knew the poem, but it is a fact that the flags of almost all the early Zionist associations borrowed the blue stripes of the tallit. A blue-and-white flag was raised over the agricultural village of Rishon Lezion in 1885 to celebrate the third anniversary of its founding. Independently of the Rishon Lezion event, a blue-and-white flag was raised in 1891 in Boston at the dedication of the meeting hall of the Bnai

Zion Educational Society. That flag had blue stripes above and below a Star of David that had the Hebrew word "Maccabee" inscribed in its center. Bnai Zion first displayed their banner publicly in October 1892, during festivities to mark the fourth centenary of the discovery of America. This time the word "Zion" replaced "Maccabee."

Flag of the Bnai Zion Educational Society in Boston, 1892 The blue stripes of the Zionist flag serve as a counterweight to the message of the Star of David. They give the flag the religious and ritual aspect totally absent from the latter. Whether the symbolic meaning of the blue stripes was perceived consciously or not, their origin in the tallit reminds onlookers of the Torah commandments. The Zionist flag uses the Star of David to express Jewish unity, which is in turn guided by the precepts of the Torah, as represented by the blue stripes and white background.

XX. Purim

One of the most festive and popular of the Jewish holidays, Purim celebrates the deliverance of the Jews from their imminent doom at the hands of their enemies in the biblical Book of Esther.

When

Purim is celebrated on the 14th day of the Hebrew month of Adar, which usually falls sometime in February or March. If it's a Jewish leap year and there is an Adar I and Adar II, the holiday falls in Adar II and Purim Katan falls in Adar I.

Purim is such a popular holiday that the ancient rabbis declared that it alone would continue to be celebrated after the Messiah comes (Midrash Mishlei 9). All other holidays will not be celebrated in the messianic days.

Purim is so-called because the villain of the story, Haman, cast the "pur" (the lot) against the Jews yet failed to destroy them. Reading Purim Story is a central part of the Purim celebration.

Reading the Megillah on Purim

The most important Purim custom is reading the Purim Story from the Scroll of Esther, also called the Megillah.

Jews usually attend synagogue for this special reading. Whenever Haman (the villain's) name is mentioned people will boo, howl, hoot and shake noisemakers (groggers) to express their dislike of him. Hearing the Megillah reading is a commandment that applies to both women and men.

Purim Costumes and Carnivals

Unlike more serious synagogue occasions, both children and adults often attend the Megillah reading in costume. Traditionally people would dress up as characters from the Purim story, for example, as Esther or Mordechai. However, nowadays people enjoy dressing up as all manner of different characters: Harry Potter, Batman, wizards, you name it! The tradition of dressing up is based upon the way Esther concealed her Jewish identity at the beginning of the Purim Story. At the conclusion of the Megillah reading, many synagogues will put on plays (shpiels) that reenact the Purim Story and poke fun at the villain. Most synagogues also host Purim Carnivals.

Purim Food Customs

As with most Jewish holidays, food plays an important role in Purim. For instance, people are commanded to send mishloach manot to other Jews. Mishloach Manot are baskets filled with food and drink. According to Jewish law each mishloach manot must contain at least two different kinds of food that is ready to eat. Most synagogues will coordinate the sending of mishloach manot, but if you want to send these baskets on your own here is a helpful article.

On Purim Jews are also supposed to enjoy a festive meal, called the Purim se'udah (meal), as part of their holiday celebration. Oftentimes people will serve hamantaschen, special Purim cookies, during the dessert course. One of the most interesting commandments related to Purim has to do with drinking. According to Jewish law, adults of drinking age are supposed to get so drunk that they can't tell the difference between Mordechai (a hero in the Purim story) and Haman (the villain). Not everyone participates in this custom and recovering alcoholics and people with health problems are exempt altogether. This drinking tradition stems from the joyous nature of Purim. (Of course, it goes without saying that if you choose to participate in this custom you should drink responsibly by arranging for a safe ride after your celebrations!)

Charity on Purim

In addition to sending mishloach manot (see above), Jews are also commanded to be especially charitable during Purim. Jews will often make monetary donations to charities they support during this time or will give money to needy people.[13]

---

[13] By Ariela Pelaia

XXI. Chanukah /Chanukiah

Hanukkah (sometimes transliterated Chanukkah) is a Jewish holiday celebrated for eight days and nights. It starts on the 25th of the Jewish month of Kislev, which coincides with late November-late December on the secular calendar.

In Hebrew, the word "hanukkah" means "dedication." The name reminds us that this holiday commemorates the re-dedication of the holy Temple in Jerusalem following the Jewish victory over the Syrian-Greeks in 165 B.C.E.

The Hanukkah Story

In 168 B.C.E. the Jewish Temple was seized by Syrian-Greek soldiers and dedicated to the worship of the god Zeus. This upset the Jewish people, but many were afraid to fight back for fear of reprisals. Then in 167 B.C.E. the Syrian-Greek emperor Antiochus made the observance of Judaism an offense punishable by death. He also ordered all Jews to worship Greek gods.

Jewish resistance began in the village of Modiin, near Jerusalem.

Greek soldiers forcibly gathered the Jewish villages and told them to bow down to an idol, then eat the flesh of a pig – both practices that are forbidden to Jews. A Greek officer ordered Mattathias, a High Priest, to acquiesce to their demands, but Mattathias refused. When another villager stepped forward and offered to cooperate on Mattathias' behalf, the High

Priest became outraged. He drew his sword and killed the villager, then turned on the Greek officer and killed him too. His five sons and the other villagers then attacked the remaining soldiers, killing all of them.

Mattathias and his family went into hiding in the mountains, where other Jews wishing to fight against the Greeks joined them. Eventually they succeeded in retaking their land from the Greeks. These rebels became known as the Maccabees, or Hasmoneans.

Once the Maccabees had regained control they returned to the Temple in Jerusalem. By this time it had been spiritually defiled by being used for the worship of foreign gods and also by practices such as sacrificing swine. Jewish troops were determined to purify the Temple by burning ritual oil in the Temple's menorah for eight days. But to their dismay, they discovered that there was only one day's worth of oil left in the Temple. They lit the menorah anyway and to their surprise the small amount of oil lasted the full eight days.

This is the miracle of the Hanukkah oil that is celebrated every year when Jews light a special menorah known as a hanukkiyah for eight days. One candle is lit on the first night of Hanukkah, two on the second, and so on, until eight candles are lit.

Significance of Hanukkah

According to Jewish law, Hanukkah is one of the less important Jewish holidays. However, Hanukkah has become much more popular in modern practice because of its proximity to Christmas.
Hanukkah falls on the twenty-fifth day of the Jewish month of Kislev. Since the Jewish calendar is lunar based, every year the first day of Hanukkah falls on a different day – usually sometime between late November and late December. Because many Jews live in predominately Christian societies, over time Hanukkah has become much more festive and Christmas-like. Jewish children receive gifts for Hanukkah – often one gift for each of the eight nights of the holiday. Many parents hope that

by making Hanukkah extra special their children won't feel left out of all the Christmas festivities going on around them.

Hanukkah Traditions

Every community has its unique Hanukkah traditions, but there are some traditions that are almost universally practiced. They are: lighting the hanukkiyah, spinning the dreidel and eating fried foods.

- **Lighting the hanukkiyah:** Every year it is customary to commemorate the miracle of the Hanukkah oil by lighting candles on a hanukkiyah. The hanukkiyah is lit every night for eight nights. Learn more about the hanukkiyah in: What Is a Hanukkiyah? | How to Light the Hanukkah Menorah | Hanukkah Candle Lighting Blessings.
- **Spinning the dreidel:** A popular Hanukkah game is spinning the dreidel, which is a four-sided top with Hebrew letters written on each side. Read The Hanukkah Dreidel to learn more about the dreidel, the meaning of the letters and how to play the game. Gelt, which are chocolate coins covered with tin foil, are part of this game.
- **Eating fried foods:** Because Hanukkah celebrates the miracle of oil, it is traditional to eat fried foods such as latkes and sufganiyot during the holiday. Latkes are pancakes made out of potatoes and onions, which are fried in oil and then served with applesauce. Sufganiyot (singular: sufganiyah) are jelly-filled donuts that are fried and sometimes dusted with confectioners' sugar before eating.

XXII Messianic Symbol

The Evangelical Press News Service (EP) released an article in July of 1999 that quoted the following:

A Messianic Seal from the Christian church in ancient Jerusalem has been rediscovered after 2,000 years. This ancient symbol was found on Mount Zion. It is believed to have been created and used by the Jewish believers who called themselves Nazarenes in the first Messianic Church. Three companies -- Olim Creative Products of Tiberias, News About Israel (NAI) of Jerusalem, and Christian Floral Delivery of Colorado -- jointly announced the discovery of this ancient symbol, which has been copyrighted by NAI. It consists of three separate but integrated symbols: a menorah at the top, a star of David in the middle, and a fish at the bottom. In each of the renditions of the three-part symbol the star is created by interlacing the stand of the menorah with the tail of the fish. The Messianic Seal was found etched or inscribed on eight ancient artifacts. The artifacts were presented to Ludwig Schneider, editor in chief of NAI's magazine Israel Today, in 1990. They came from Tech Otecus, an elderly monk who lived as a hermit in the Old City of Jerusalem. Otecus said that in the 1960's he had personally excavated about 40 artifacts bearing the Messianic Seal from an ancient grotto located in the immediate vicinity of the Upper Room on Mount Zion. What was once the main entrance to the grotto is now covered with a jail-like heavy wire mesh enclosure. Its door, leading down into the ancient baptismal place, is tightly secured with a heavy chain and lock. According to Schneider, **the last remaining entry to the**

grotto was sealed shortly after he excitedly told the priests at the local monastery about the discovery of the Messianic Seal. Schneider photographed eight artifacts which were given to him by Otecus, and showed the pictures to the curator of the Israel Museum. "When he had carefully studied my pictures," Schneider recalled, "the curator immediately promised me that these artifacts and their unique symbol were an important find. He told me that the museum already had seen other artifacts bearing the same three-part symbol from some other sources he did not specify." According to Bob Fischer, president of Olim Creative Products and co-author with local historian and artist Reuven Schmalz of their book, The Messianic

Seal of the Jerusalem Church, **the ancient three-part symbol has, since 135 AD, been suppressed by various Israeli groups or agencies, such as the Israel Museum and Orthodox rabbis in the Old City of Jerusalem, while simultaneously being buried for these nearly two millennia by the church.** According to Fischer, at least two of the eight artifacts were obviously ceremonial pieces which may well have been used by James the Just, the brother of Jesus, who is said to be the first pastor of the church, or perhaps even by one or more of the Twelve Apostles. One of the eight artifacts is a brick-sized block of well-worn local marble. This piece bears an etched version of the Messianic Seal with a Taw (the last letter in the ancient Hebrew alphabet that looks exactly like a sign of the cross) in the eye of the fish symbol, as well as the ancient Aramaic lettering proclaiming the use of this artifact as a stand to hold a vial of anointing oil. The ancient Aramaic is transliterated as, "La Shemen Ruehon" **(For the Oil of the Spirit).** Another of the eight artifacts is a small, almost intact, vial which could well have sat on top of the marble stand.

Commenting on what he characterized as the "monumental importance" of this archaeological discovery, Fischer said, "**Beyond the historical background of the Nazarenes, the first Jewish believers who founded the Jerusalem Church, the Messianic Seal itself proclaims to the world the pervasive Jewishness of Jesus Christ and the decidedly Jewish foundation and roots of the church founded in His name.** The Messianic Seal of the Jerusalem Church," Fischer continued, "strikes at the very roots of anti-Semitism while proclaiming a compelling message that restores unity: Jew with Jew, and Jew with Gentile. The importance of this discovery cannot be minimized. The Messianic Seal is not only just the key to understanding the Dead Sea Scrolls, **it can and should shake the foundations of the church and orthodox Judaism with its incredible message of unity and love. It breaks down barriers that have existed for millennia and points the way toward restoration.**"

XXIII Messianic Terminology

A

Abba
Means 'father' sometimes seen as simply ab. Used in numerous phrases and constructions, such as ab bet din (lit. "father of/in the house of judgment") for one of the presiders in the Jewish sanhedrin

Abraham (Avraham)
(adj. Abrahamic). The patriarch who is acknowledged as the father of the Jewish people. Presumed to have lived sometime in the period 2000-1700 B.C.; father of Ishmael by Hagar and of Isaac by Sarah. See Bible Genesis 12-25; New Testament Galatians 3-4.

Abwehr
Intelligence services of the Wehrmacht. Most of their activities were gradually taken over by the SS, being absorbed by it in 1944.

Acacia Tortilis (The Umbrella Tree)
A tree prevalent in the southern wadis (valleys) of Israel.
Produces a large number of pods that are eaten by wild and domestic animals, and sometimes by man. The pods are tightly coiled spirals, pale brown and fall to the ground unopened. They accumulate in large numbers and are eaten with relish by such animals as kudu, impala, rhino and elephant. This is the manner in which the seeds of the unopened pod are dispersed for propagation and better germination after passing through an animal's stomach. The pods of some other acacia trees split before falling to the ground, thus dispersing the seeds by scattering.

Acharit HaYamim
'End of days'

Adonai
'Lord'

Adon Olam
There are different versions of it including a Chasidik version. What it is
is a liturgical hym depicting the unity and providence of G-d. it's usually
recited at the beginning and end of the service and also at one's deathbed.
It's origin isn't known exactly but traditionally it's ascribed to Solomon
ibn Gabirol. Click on the play button on the right to hear it.

Afikomen
'dessert' -- it contains a broken piece of matzah and is hidden during the
Passover seder only to be brought out at the end of the meal (hence
'dessert').

Alephbet
The Hebrew alphabet -- 'aleph' is first letter of alphabet, 'bet' is second.

Aliyah
To immigrate to the land of Israel, also being called to read from Torah at
shul or to recite the blessing.

Amain
Same as Amen (Some prefer Omein)

Amidah
'Standing' prayer that originally consisted of 18 benedictions, but
interestingly, a 19th malediction (a curse) was added to the Amidah,
intended (supposedly) as a jab against Jews who believed in Yeshua as
messiah, since it cursed 'heretics' to traditional Judaism.

Aninut
Mourning period immediately following burial.

Anomianism
'Lawlessness' that is, 'without Torah' or 'having no Torah.'

Antisemitism
Literally means 'against the Semites' which includes all Semitic peoples, but today used mostly to describe hatred and crimes against the Jewish people.

Apocrypha
Books included in the Septuagint and Vulgate but excluded from Jewish and Protestant canons of the Old Testament.

Aramaic
A Semitic language known since the ninth century B.C.; official language of the Persian empire; used extensively in southwest Asia and by the Jews after the Babylonian exile; the cursive script replaced the ancient paleo-Hebrew script for secular writing as well as for holy scriptures.

Ashkenazi
Eastern and central European Jews also, Jews from France; Ashkenazi have customs that differ from Sephardic Jews.

B

Baptism
Many Messianics do not use this term. We refer to believer's immersion or mikva. Baptism again is associated with the "forced conversions and baptisms," perpetrated against Jewish people by anti-Semites of the past, who did these things in the Name of Jesus. We seek to refer to the Messianic MIKVAH, the immersion of believers, which had its origin in Jewish practice. Our purpose in this is to emphasize the true Jewish roots of our faith, and

separate ourselves from those people and their
actions who profaned the name of the Messiah by
their deeds which were CONTRARY to His teaching.
Baptism is an integral part of the New Birth described in God's New
Covenant Scriptures. Two types of baptism are described - baptism in
water and baptism in the Holy Spirit (Ruach HaKodesh).

Bar Kochba Simeon ben Kozeba
Led a Jewish revolt against Rome in 132 CE, the name means 'son of a
star.' Messianic Jews did not participate in this revolt since traditional
Jews considered Bar Kochbar a Messianic figure. This refusal of
Messianic Jews to participate in this revolt caused a further breakdown of
relations between Jewish believers and traditional Jews.

Bar Mitzvah
Non-Scriptural rite of passage, literally means "Son of the
Commandment" and is achieved at age 13 when a boy reaches an age of
responsibility towards G-d's Torah. Originated in the Talmudic age and
became a popularized ritual in the 16th and 17th centuries.

Bat Mitzvah
Non-Scriptural rite of passage, literally means "Daughter of the
Commandment" and is achieved at age 12 when a girl reaches an age of
responsibility towards G-d's Torah. First known Bat Mizvah occured in
1921 for Judith Kaplan, the daughter of Reconstuctionist movement
founder, Mordecai Kaplan.

Baruch
'Blessed' (Blessings begin 'Baruch atah adonai....').

Baruchot/Berachot
Blessings (formal)

B.C.E.
Before the Common Era; indicates that a time division falls before the Christian era; It means the same thing as B.C. but many Jews don't like to say BC as it means "Before Christ"

Beit Din
This is a court established to resolve issues within G-d's community -- the first known Messianic Beit Din was in Jerusalem, headed by the Apostle James.

Beit Midrash
Literally means "House of Study"

Believer
Many Messianics use this term instead of the term "Christian." Many Jews consider"Christians" to be those people who hate and persecuted the Jewish people for two millennia. "Christian" is used only twice in the New Covenant Scriptures. An earlier term is Believers, and can be used generically of those who are Messianic as well as those who are in traditional churches, who TRULY believe in Yeshua and seek to follow Him. By using the term "believer," we are focusing on a person's having made a commitment to follow the L-rd
and not bringing in the excess baggage of those who called themselves "Christians" but did not walk as He walked.

Binyan Av
Rabbinic argument style where a foundational passage serves to interpret other passages.

Blintz
A crepe-like treat filled with cheese or fruits.

B'nei Noach
Gentiles who reject Yeshua, but choose to obey the 7 laws of Noah as interpreted by traditional rabbis rather than committing to full conversion to Judaism and receiving whole Torah.

Brit Chadasha
'New Covenant' aka New Testament.

Brit Milah (Bris)
The 'Covenant of Circumcision' as given to Abraham, performed on the 8th day by all of Abraham's descendants. Brit Milah is also practiced as part of the conversion ritual to Judaism, a practice which dates back to the Pharisees.

C

Calendar
The Biblical calendar is lunar-based and its months were generally referred to numerically (1st month, 2nd month etc.). The modern Jewish calendar was influenced by the Babylonian calendar and some month names are Babylonian in origin. The only months mentioned by their Hebrew names in Scripture are: Aviv, Ziv, Sivan, Elul, Ethanim, Bul, Chisleu, Tevet, Shevat, and Adar. Other month names, like Nisan (which replaces biblical Aviv), Tammuz, Av, Iyyar (which replaces biblical Ziv), Heshvan (which replaces biblical Bul) and Tishri (which replaces biblical Ethanim) are borrowed from the Babylonian calendar.

Canon:
a collection of books accepted as holy scripture.

CE 'Common Era' -
used in place of 'AD' by traditional Jews because 'AD' means 'the Year of Our L-rd' and reckons time by the birth of Yeshua. See BCE above for further explanation

Chachkas
Yiddish for bric-a-brac

Chag Sameach A greeting used to mean 'Happy Holiday' during the festivals. Can be personalized for the specific moedim: Chag Pesakh, Chag Sukkot, etc.

Chai Means 'life' -- a popular greeting is 'L'chayim' meaning 'to life.' In Jewish mysticism, the numeric value of words are often added up to find hidden meanings in words. The letters comprising "Chai' equal a total of 18, hence the practice of giving money and donations in increments of 18 dollars.

Challah A braided sweet egg bread served traditionally in a loaf shape for the weekly shabbat and served in a round shape for Rosh Hoshana.

Chametz Means 'leaven' which is forbidden during Pesakh (Passover) and Chag HaMatzah (Unleavened Bread).

Chanukah Means "Festival of Dedication" and commemorates both the battle triumph of the Maccabees in recapturing Jerusalem and the temple, as well the miracle of the olive oil burning for 8 straight days in the temple following this victory.

Chanukiah The 9-branched menorah used at Chanukah, as opposed to the biblical 7-branched menorah.

Charoset Traditionally, this is mixture of apples, raisons, nuts and wine served at Pesakh (Passover) to represent mortar on the seder plate.

Chasidic A sect of Orthodox Judaism.

Chaver, Chaverim Chaver means 'friend' -- Chaverim is plural, 'friends.'

Chol v'chomer Popular rabbinic argument style found in many Jewish writings, including Brit Chadasha (New Testament) meaning from lesser to greater (or greater to lesser) "If this .... then how much more so..."

Cholent A traditional stew that is kept warm to avoid cooking on Shabbat.

Chukkim Torah commands whose reasons aren't fully explained in Torah -- we obey them without understanding their purpose simply because G-d commanded us to.

Chumash Means 'five' and is a book which includes all the Torah Parshot and Haftorah readings.

Chuppah The canopy which the bride and groom stand under

Churban - destruction or disaster. Frequently used in the phrase "First Churban" to refer to the events relating to the Babylonian exile and in the phrase "Second Churban" to refer to the destruction of Jerusalem and the death of 1,100,000 Jews following a siege by the Roman general Titus.

Circumcision Foreskin removal -- the commandment was given by G-d to Abraham; to this day obeyed by the children of Isaac and Ishmael.

Cohen Means 'Priest' -- a descendant of Aaron the Levite and responsible for temple service.

Commandments The Torah instructions, the rabbis counted 613 commandments in all -- these include the decalogue (aka 'ten commandments).

Congregation: We do not refer to our congregations as

"Churches." Churches are associated with anti-Semitism by Jewish people because in the past, and in some places today, anti-Semitism has come from those who profess to be believers and even from the clergy. Ecclesia refers more to the people than the building, and "Congregation" does just that. A synonym in the New Covenant for "ekklesia" is "sunagoge'" as it is used in James 2:1-6, referring to a meeting of believers. We therefore use Congregation or Synagogue in place of Church.

Conversion: A Born Again beliver in Yeshua does not need to convert to Messianic Judaism but it is nessacery for a non believer to convert to Christianity or Messiaqnic Judaism

Counting of the Omer Counting the days between Pesakh (Passover) and Shavuot (Pentecost).

Covenant: This is a reference to Testament. Instead of old Testament and New Testament, we refer to them as Old Covenant and New Covenant. It is also a legal agreement between God and Israel. The Sinaitic Covenant is frequently termed Torah.

Cross: Many Mesianics avoid the symbol of the CROSS. To Jewish people it is a symbol of persecution in Jesus' Name.

D

Davar Halameid Mi'Inyano
Rabbinic argument style where one verse is understood by the context of total passage

Daven
A style of prayer, a kind of rocking back and forth while praying (see animation on right)

Days of Awe
Traditionally, the ten days following Rosh Hoshana and preceding Yom Kippur; aka "Ten Days of Awe." This is a time to examine one's life, make peace, seek forgiveness and make amends for all the wrongs committed in the previous year.

Diaspora
The dispersion of the Jewish people to lands outside of Israel. Also often called the Galut or the Exile. Exile is a Sinaitic Covenant judgement (see Vayikra/Leviticus 26:33 and Dvarim/Deuteronomy 28:64

Dispensationalism
Relatively new church doctrine which divides G-d's Plan up into two separate dispensations; it pits Torah against Grace; an age of Israel against a church age. Basically, Dispensationalism creates a confused G-d and confused followers. It leads to anomianism (lawlessness) and pre-tribulational eschatology scenarios to accommodate G-d's supposed 'two sets of people.' Dispensationalists read the bible in terms of 'this applies to me, this doesn't apply to me' instead of acknowledging G-d has One Way for *all* His children.

Dreidel
A Chanukah game using a spinning top containing the Hebrew alephbet letters: Nun, Gimmel, Hey, and Shin. These letters stand for nes godal hayah sham ("a great miracle happened there"); but in Israel, the 'Shin' is changed to 'Peh' so it will stand for "a great miracle happened here."

E

Ein Sof
Means 'unending' -- in Jewish mysticism represents the essense of the infinite G-d.

Elohim
Means 'G-d,' 'gods,' and 'judges.'

Essenes
A sect of Judaism begun a couple hundred years before Yeshua --- the Dead Sea Scrolls found at Qumran were Essene manuscripts.

Ethics Of The Sages/Fathers
Rabbinic writing known as "Pirke Avot", traditionally studied between Pesakh (Passover) and Shavuot (Pentecost).

Etrog
Citris fruit used during festival of Sukkot.

Eyshet Chayil/Eshet Chayil
Means 'woman of valor' as taught in Proverbs 31:10-31

F

Fleishig (or basar)
Means 'meat' in Yiddish. According to rabbinic Judaism, dairy products cannot be used with meat products, so kitchen utensils are kept separate to designate if they are for dairy (milchig) or meat (fleishig).

G

Galut - The dispersion of Jews from the land of Israel. Also often called the Diaspora or the Exile. Exile is a Sinaitic Covenant judgement (see Vayikra/Leviticus 26:33 and Dvarim/Deuteronomy 28:64.

Gefilte Fish
Stuffed Fish dish. Tastes great but you don't want to know what's in it.

Gemara
Commentaries on the Mishneh --
the Mishneh and Commentaries together form the Talmud. The Mishna was in place when Yeshua was here and he believed it should be followed but later there were additions made to it that are not sanctioned by Him

Gematria
Kabbalist numerology which seeks out hidden meanings in words based on the numeric value of its letters.

Gentiles
Goyim (pl) Goy (sing) for nations.

Get
A divorce decree given to the wife, aka sefer kritut.

Gezeirah Shavah
Rabbinic style argument by analogy -- comparing similar words in different Scriptural passages.

Glatt Kosher
Means 'smooth' -- referring to the smooth lungs of a non-diseased kosher animal slaughtered. It doesn't mean 'extra kosher' or 'premium kosher' as some misuse the term.

Goy/Goyim
Means 'nations,' sometimes translated "gentiles.' Common usage today is as a 'non-Jew,' however, Israel itself is a goy/nation: "And ye shall be unto me a kingdom of priests, and an holy nation (Strong's 01471 - 'goy)'. Exodus 19:6a

Grogger
Noisemaker used during Purim whenever Haman's name is mentioned.

Gut Shabbes/Gut Shabbos
Greeting of "Shabbat Shalom" (Peaceful Sabbath) in Yiddish as "Good Sabbath."

H

Haftarah
Weekly reading from the Prophets, read in addition to Torah Parsha.

Haggadah
Means 'the telling' of the Exodus, it codifies the order of the Pesakh meal (seder).

Halachah
Means 'the way to walk' and are rabbinic interpretations of how Torah is to be obeyed.

Hallel
Songs of praise found in Psalms 113-118 and read on Pesakh (Passover).

Haman
Evil high ranking official in King Ahasuerus's court who tried to get the king to exterminate all the Jews in the land. Through G-d's provision, the Jews were able to survive this attempt.

Hamentaschen
A triangular dessert cookie served at Purim.

Hamesh/Hamsa Hand Hamesh/Hamsa
means 'five.' In Jewish mysticism, this was an amulet to protect its wearer
from the evil eye.

Hanukah/Hanukkah
Means "Festival of Dedication" and commemorates both the battle
triumph of the Maccabees in recapturing Jerusalem and the temple, as
well the miracle of the olive oil burning for 8 straight days in the temple
following this victory.

HaShem
'The Name.'

Havdalah
Means 'separation.' An traditional observance marking the end of the
weekly Shabbat/Sabbath with wine and spices.

I

J

Jesus -
The English version of the Greek name IESOUS, itself a form of the
Hebrew/Aramaic Yeshua or Yehoshua, meaning salvation.

Jew
Means 'Praiser' -- comes from 'Judah. Today means those from tribes of
Judah, Levi, Benjamin and others who returned to Israel following
Babylonian captivity.

Jewish Law
Includes the Ten Commandments, the Torah, the Old Testament and the Oral Law or any combination of these.

K

Kabbalah
Book of Jewish Mysticism. It dabbles in witchcraft

Kashrut
Means 'proper' and refers to Kosher dietary laws.

Kavanah
Means 'intention'

Kelal Ufrat
A rabbinic argument style where a general summary statement is followed by an explanatory, more specific statement.

Ketubah
A traditional Jewish marriage contract

Kethuvim/Ketuvim
The Writings, the section of the TaNaKh containing: Psalms, Proverbs, Job, Song of Songs, Ruth, Lamentations, Ecclesiastes, Esther, Daniel, Ezra, Nehemiah, and The Chronicles.

Ke Yotzei Bo Mimakom Acher "Like it says elsewhere" Rabbinic argument style where the explanation of a word in one text is clarified by use of same word in an unrelated text.

Kiddush
Prayer of santification recited over a cup of wine to consecrate the Sabbath or a festival

Kippah Aka Yarmulke -- this is the skullcap worn by Jews, the cap is a fairly recent non-Scriptural tradition.

Kittel White garments for burial, sometimes worn also for Yom Kippur services.

Kli Gever Refers to the prohibition against the dress and habits of the other sex

Knaidelach Matzo balls

Knish Stuffed potato and flour dumpling.

Kohen/Kohanim Means 'Priest' -- a descendant of Aaron the Levite and responsible for temple service.

Kol Nidre The prayer that begins the Yom Kippur service.

Kosher Foods that Torah permits man to eat are kosher. Used loosely to mean anything permissible for G-d's people.

Kugel Seasoned pudding made from noodles or potatoes.

L

Lag b'Omer Means the 33rd day of the Omer since in jewish mysticism the sum letter totals of "lamud" and "gimmel" in 'Lag' equal 33. Tradition teaches that during the destruction of the second temple, many of Rabbi Akiva's students were dying of an epidemic, but on this day, the epidemic creased and students lived. In commemoration, this day is a day of rejoicing.

Latkes Fried potato pancakes eaten during Chanukah with applesauce or sour cream on top.

Lashon Hara Means 'evil tongue' and is a prohibition against harmful speech against others

L'Chayim From 'Chai' meaning 'life' -- this popular greeting means 'to life.' In Jewish mysticism, the numeric value of words are often added up to find hidden meanings in words. The letters comprising "Chai" equal a total of 18, hence the practice of giving money and donations in increments of 18 dollars.

Leap Year Due to differences in year length between the modern solar calendar year and the Biblical lunar calendar year, a leap year is added to realign the calendars.

L'hitraot Means 'see you' used instead of goodbye or shalom in a more casual 'see you soon' sort of way.

Lox Smoked salmon

L'Shanah Tovah Means 'for a good year' and is a popular greeting at Rosh Hashana.

Lulav This is the palm branch waved during Sukkot (Festival of Tabernacles/Booths)

M

Machzor A prayerbook used during the high Holy Days.

Magen David/Mogen David Six-pointed star of David used as symbol of Jewishness today. Somewhat dubious history with pagan origins; first Jewish use was in 13th century Prague and later adopted by Zionist mov't in the 19th century. While Nazis forced Jewish people to wear the star, today the star's popularity is such that it's become the symbol of Jewishness worldwide.

Maimonides The famous Jewish scholar/author Rabbi Moshe ben Maimon (1135-1204) better known as 'Rambam.'

Mashiach/Moshiach Means 'annointed' and translated as Messiah or Christ.

Matzah Unleavened bread eaten during Pesakh (Passover) which Yeshua used to designate His body at the last Pesakh seder (Last Supper) prior to His crucifixion.

Matzah Ball Soup This is a soup that uses matzah balls (matzah meal, egg, oil, seasonings) in a chicken broth; can be made with or without added vegetables.

Matzah Meal Crumbs from crushed matzah bread; used as a flour or for breading.

Mazel Tov Means 'good star' or 'good constellation' and comes from Jewish mysticism; commonly used today as 'congratulations.'

Mechitzah In strict congregations, this is a curtain or partition between men's and women's sections at the synagogue or other religions functions.

Megillah Means 'scroll' -- can refer to any of five books of Scripture: Ruth, Song of Songs, Esther, Lamentations or Ecclesiastes but most commonly used during Purim, referring to the Megillah of Esther.

Menorah The seven-branched candlestick G-d commanded the Israelites to make.

Messiah Means 'annointed' and comes from the Hebrew word 'mashiach.' Yeshua was the Messiah foretold in the TaNaKh.

We often use this term instead of "Christ". Christ is derived from the greek word meaning Anointed One. By using the Hebrew term rather than the Greek, we are again, emphasizing that the Messiah is for Jewish people, and not exclusively for Gentiles. A secondary reason is because many countless thousands and perhaps millions of Jewish people have been persecuted and butchered in the name of Christ. Christ carries a non-Jewish, as well as anti-Jewish connotation to many Jewish people.

Messianic: This refers to those believers who are involved in a Messianic congregation, whether Jewish or Gentile. All are Messianic believers, but Messianic Jews, are those in such congregations who are of Jewish descent. Messianic refers to that expression of the Biblical faith which expresses itself in a Jewish manner.

Messianic Age A thousand year period where Yeshua will rule the earth as its king. Israel and Judah will be reunited, the temple will be rebuilt, the resurrection will occur, there will be peace on earth.

Messianic Judaism: A worldwide movement of Jewish people who believe that Yeshua is the promised Jewish Messiah and Saviour for Israel and the world. Messianic Judaism depends entirely on the Scriptures.

Messianic Jew: A Jew who believes that Yeshua is the Messiah AND remains Jewish in lifestyle and worship.

Mezuzah Means 'doorpost' -- this is a rabbinic tradition where a miniature scroll is affixed to a doorway. The mezuzah contains two verses inside it, Deuteronomy 6:4-9 and 11:13-21. G-d instructs us in these two passages to "Lay up these my words in your heart and in your soul, and bind them for a sign upon your hand, that they may be as frontlets between your eyes. And ye shall teach them your children, speaking of them when thou sittest in thine house, and when thou walkest by the way, when thou liest down, and when thou risest up. And thou shalt write them upon the door posts of thine house, and upon thy gates." "These words" refer to His Torah. Yet ironically, the mezuzah doesn't put the actual Torah on doorposts, instead it mocks the command by merely parroting the command that we should put Torah on our doorposts. Oy. Further, if we take this command literally, we also need to surgically put a mezuzah in our heart and soul, and add one to fenceposts as well. Clearly the verse is meant to say "Keep My Torah inside of you and around you always and teach It to your children so they will do the same."

Midrash Means 'study'

Mikveh Means 'gathering' and was a ritual bath used achieve ritual cleanliness by priests. Later rabbinic writings associated this ritual bath with female cleanliness following her menstrual cycles; mikveh is also used for female conversions in modern Judaism. At the time of Yeshua, mikveh was used to identify one's religious affiliations and to renew one's faith -- baptism itself is a type of mikveh.

Milchig Means 'dairy' in Yiddish. According to rabbinic Judaism dairy products cannot be used with meat products, kitchen utensils are kept separate to designate if they are for dairy (milchig) or meat (fleishig). The actual command in Scripture in Exodus 34:26b reads: "Thou shalt not seethe a kid in his mother's milk." It is from this passage the rabbis interpreted that no meat should be consumed with dairy.

Minyan Means 'number' and refers to the necessary quorum for religious services (which is ten adult men).

Mishneh Rabbinic writings codified about 200 CE.

Mitzvah/Mitzvot Means 'commandment' -- used to mean any commandment or good deed one might perform.

Moedim Holy Days -- G-d's appointed times.

Mohel The one who performs the circumcision on an eight day old male baby.

Mosaic: Comes from the name Moshe (Moses). We at Mosaic Ministries call ourselves "Mosaic Jews". We feel that the term Messianic is being used to describe Saved Jews who do not follow G-d's Laws along with those who do follow G-d's commandents. Mosaic Jew describes us better and allows others to know exactly who we are.

Mysticism Mysticism became markedly important in rabbinic Judaism following the Babylonian captivity. Astrology, numerology, and general interest in the occult flourished. Today most evidenced by Kabbalistic studies.

N

Ner Tamid Means 'eternal light' -- symbolizes the menorah that burned constantly in the temple.

New Covenant - A legal agreement by God with the house of Israel and the house of Judah which became necessary when the Covenant made at Sinai was broken repeatedly. It is described briefly in Yirmiyahu/Jeremiah 31:29-37, Yechezkiel/Ezekiel 18 and also in God's New Covenant (Testament) Scriptures.

Nevi'im The Prophets, the section of the TaNaKh containing: Joshua, Judges, Books of Samuel, Books of Kings, Isaiah, Jeremiah, Ezekiel, Hosea, Joel, Amos, Obadiah, Jonah, Micah, Nahum, Habakkuk, Zephaniah, Haggai, Zechariah, and Malachi.

Niddah The laws governing separation of man and wife during her menstrual cycle.

Noahic Commandments (Noachide Laws) Seven commandments the rabbis interpret as governing all mankind, Jew and non-Jew alike. A promise made by God to mankind generally (see Genesis 9:8-17. A later fabrication is also sometimes referred to by the same term but the fabricated content is not mentioned in the authentic description of the Noachide Covenant.

O

Olam Haba Means 'the world to come' and refers to the Messianic age when Yeshua will rule and peace will abound.

Old Testament Using Septuagint book ordering, this is the Christian "TaNaKh."

Omer Means 'sheaf' and used a unit of measure in Scripture.

Onah Sex for recreational pleasure instead of pru u'rvu (procreation)

Oneg Shabbat Means 'Sabbath Delight' -- this is a celebration occuring after services at many synagogues on Shabbat.

Oral Torah/Oral Law These are traditional writings written by rabbis and scribes. Considered by traditional/rabbinic Judaism to be as inspired as Scripture itself, called the Talmud, which consists of Mishneh and its commentaries (Gemara). Messianic Judaism does not consider the oral tradition equal to the Bible.

Orthodox Strictest sect of Judaism, devotes tremendous amount of study not only to Torah and Talmud, but to Jewish mysticism (Kabbalah) also.

P

PRDS PaRDes Four rabbinic levels of Torah understanding: Pashat-simple; Remez-hint; Drash-search; Sod-hidden

Parah Adumah Red heifer mentioned in Numbers 19 -- the ashes of this heifer were for purifying purposes.

Pareve (parve) Means 'neutral' and refers to foods that contain neither meat or dairy products.

Parsha The weekly Torah readings read at shul and studied at home.

Pasach
The major Jewish spring holiday (with agricultural aspects) also known as hag hamatzot (festival of unleavened bread) commemorating the Exodus or deliverance of the Hebrew people from Egypt (see Exodus 12-13). The festival lasts eight days, during which Jews refrain from eating all leavened foods and products. A special ritual meal called the Seder is prepared, and a traditional narrative called the Haggadah, supplemented by hymns and songs, marks the event.

Passover (see Pasach directly above)

Patriarchs Refers to Abraham, Isaac and Jacob -- forefathers of the Jewish people.

Pentecost Greek for 'fifty' and is the festival of Shavuot -- this was when the Ruach (Holy Spirit) fell on the apostles in Jerusalem.

Peyot The side locks (hair) worn by Orthodox men, a relatively new practice begun a couple hundred years ago by the Chasidic Jews.

Pharisees/P'rushim Ancestor to modern day rabbinic Judaism -- this sect of Judaism was flourishing at the time of Yeshua -- they put great importance on the oral tradition. After the destruction of the temple, most other sects of Judaism died out, leaving Pharisaic Judaism to dominate.

Phylacteries These are leather boxes containing scrolls with Scripture passages, the rabbis interpreted G-d's command to wear His Word on hands and forehead -- for more info, see Mezuzah.

Pirkei Avot Also known as "Ethics of the Sages/Fathers," this is a rabbinic tractate traditionally studied between (Passover) and Shavuot (Pentecost).

Pneuma Means 'the wind' 'to breathe' or 'blow' -- Greek for 'Spirit'

Pru u'rvu Sex for procreation purposes as opposed to onah (recreational, sexual pleasure)

Purim Means 'lots' and is the celebration of Jewish victory after the failed attempt to exterminate Jews from Persia -- story found in scroll of Esther.

Q

R

Rabbi Means 'teacher' but modern Judaism tends to require a degree or some sort of certification -- a knowledgeable layman generally won't earn such a title anymore.

Rabbinic Judaism: Judaism centered around Rabbininc writings and teachings. Birthed in 70 A.D. after the destruction of the Second Temple. Prior to that Judaism was centered around the Temple and the Torah, The Law of the five books of Moses. After the destruction the Rabbis reorganized Judaism introducing many new laws, traditions and rules into what has become the Talmud. There are many branches of Rabbinic Judaism, Orthodox, Chassidic, Reform, Conservative and Reconstructionist.

Rambam Famous Jewish scholar/author Rabbi Moshe ben Maimon (1135-1204) also known as 'Maimonides.' You may already be familiar with his: Thirteen Articles of the Jewish Faith and Eight Levels of Charity

Rashi Famous bible commentator, Rabbi Shlomo Yitzchaki (1040-1105 CE).

Rebbetzin Means the wife of a rabbi

Reconstructionism Founded by Mordecai M. Kaplan (1881-1983), it Defines itself as an evolving and more dynamic Judaism.

Red Heifer (Parah Adumah) Red heifer mentioned in Numbers 19 -- the ashes of this heifer were for purifying purposes.

Reform Founded by Rabbi Isaac Mayer Wise, this is a more progressive sect in Judaism, more liberal in its treatment of women and more liberal in its conversion requirements.

Reincarnation Reincarnation is taught in the Talmud as Din Gilgol Neshomes, meaning '"the judgment of the revolutions of the souls." This is another reason why Talmud is not considered on par with Scripture by Messianics.

Repentance - A recognition of and turning away from past sin against God. It includes both a change of attitude and, if genuine, a change of behaviour.

Replacement Theology False church doctrine which teaches the church replaces Israel in G-d's Plan. Basically all the blessings promised to Israel are usurped by the church (though the replacement theologists generally allow Israel to keep all the curses she was promised -- Oy!).

Rosh Chodesh Means 'head of the month' -- the new month begins when the first sliver of the new moon is seen.

Rosh Hashana Traditional Judaism refers to Rosh Hashana as the 'new year' but this is actually inaccurate from a Scriptural point of view. In Scripture, Rosh Hashana (or "Feast of Trumpets/Shofar") occurs in the seventh month, not the first month. It is not the new year at all according to biblical year reckoning.

Ruach Means 'Spirit' from Hebrew for 'wind, breath, air, strength, breeze.'

Ruach Elohim - One of the phrases used in the Hebrew text of the Tanakh to refer to the Holy Spirit.

Ruach HaKodesh Means 'Holy Spirit'

Ruach Yahveh - Holy Spirit. Ruach Yahveh is the most common term explicitly used in the Hebrew text of the Tanakh to refer to the Holy Spirit.

S

Sabbath From 'Shabbat' -- G-d blessed and sanctified the seventh day of the week as a day of rest.

Sacrifice Modern Judaism doesn't offer sacrifices since the temple has been destroyed; but Messianics view Yeshua as sin sacrifice.

Sadducees This sect of Judaism died out with the loss of the temple in 70CE, since their whole belief revolved around temple work, and not oral tradition.

Sages Refers to the great Jewish scholars whose work is preserved still this day in oral tradition.

Sandek The person who holds the baby during his circumcision -- often the child's grandfather.

Second Churban - The destruction of Jerusalem which resulted in the deaths of some 1,100,000 Jews at the hands of the forces of the Roman Empire and was the beginning of an exile lasting over 1,800 years.

Seder Means 'order' and is usually used to refer to the Pesakh dinner using the Haggadah as a guide.

Sefer Means 'book' -- can be used generically for any religious books, or used more specifically as in "Sefer Torah" (books of Torah) or "Sefer Yetzirah" (book of creation).

Sefer Kritut Means 'cutting off the book/writing' -- a divorce decree given to the wife, aka a 'get.'

Sefirot In Jewish mysticism (according to Kabbalah) there are ten Sefirot or Divine Emanations of G-d.

Selichot These are special prayers for forgiveness recited on fast days.

Sephardic Jews Jews from Spain, Portugal, Africa and middle eastern countries.

Septuagint LXX Means 'seventy' for the seventy scribes who translated the Torah into Greek around 3nd century BC; the Writings and Prophets were translated later, 2nd century BC.

Shabbat Means 'sabbath' G-d blessed and sanctified the seventh day of the week as a day of rest

Shabbat Shalom Means 'peaceful sabbath' -- a common greeting when Shabbat is approaching.

Shalom Means 'peace' but also used as a greeting to say hello or goodbye.

Shalom Aliechem Means 'peace to you' or 'peace unto you' -- a greeting.

Shalom Bayit/Shalom Bayis Means having/maintaining peace within the home.

Shammus Means 'servant' and is the candle used to light other candles in menorah; also, a synagogue custodian.

Shavua Tov Means 'good week' and is a popular greeting when shabbat ends.

Shavuot Means 'weeks' -- known in Greek as Pentecost.

Shehitah Means 'slaughter' and refers to kosher slaughtering of animals.

Sheitels Yiddish for 'wigs'

Shekinah/Shechinah (-h also) Means 'divine presence of G-d' -- a term frequently bandied about by Messianics who do not realize the word appears no where in Scripture and comes straight from the Kabbalah rooted in Jewish mysticism.

Shema Means 'hear' and is the quintessential Jewish text from Dvarim/Deuteronomy 6:4.: "Hear, O Israel: The LORD our God is one LORD" showing the uniqueness of the G-d of Israel. Israel didn't require many gods (like harvest gods, fertility gods, fire gods) The G-d of Israel is unique and infinite -- He alone is sovereign.
The Shema is a confirmation in Torah that Yahveh is a compound unity ("echad") not as is commonly misunderstood.

Shemoneh Esrei "Standing" prayer that originally consisted of 18 benedictions, but interestingly, a 19th malediction (a curse) was added to the Shemoneh Esrei intended (supposedly) as a jab against Jews who believed in Yeshua as messiah, since it cursed 'heretics' to traditional Judaism

Sh'enei Ketuvim Rabbinic argument style where two laws that seem to contradict are settled by another verse which resolves the conflict.

Shiva Means 'seven' and refers to the one week period of mourning following the death of a family member.

Shloshim Means 'thirty' and refers to the one month period of mourning following the death of a family member.

Shoah - The Holocaust.

Shochet Person who butchers kosher animals.

Shofar Ram's horn, also translated 'trumpet' in some bibles.

Shul Synagogue in Yiddish.

Siddur Prayer book

Simchat Torah Means rejoicing in Torah and celebrates the ending and beginning of the Torah parshot annual reading cycle.

Sinaitic Covenant - A legal agreement made between Yahveh the God of Avraham, Yitzak and Yaaqov at Sinai. The Sinaitic Covenant included obligations on God and obligations on the Israelite community.

Sukkah Means 'booth' and translated 'tabernacles' in some bibles. Shaul the tentmaker may have been a sukkah maker.

Sukkot Means 'booths' -- this is the festival of tabernacles which commemorates G-d's protection on Israel when she lived in tents under His protection.

Synagogue From the Greek synagogia, this is a meeting place for assembly.

T

Tabernacles From 'sukkot' means 'booths' -- this is the festival of tabernacles which commemorates G-d's protection on Israel when she lived in tents under His protection.

Taharat HaMishpachah Family purity laws which govern the separation of a man and his wife during her menstrual cycle.

Tallit Prayer shawl with tzitzit (fringed edges), based on the command in Numbers 15:38 and Deuteronomy 22:12 that men wear Tzitzit on their garments. The prayer shawl is a rabbinic compromise to this law since a tallit isn't quite a garment, but it does contain tzitzit.

Tallit Katan Closer to a garment than the regular prayer shawl, this is worn under clothing and contains the commanded tzitzit.

Talmud The collection of oral tradition: the Mishneh and Gemara/commentaries.

TaNaKh/Tenach/TNK Jewish Scriptures, divided into three sections: Torah, Nevi'im (prophets) , and Ketubim or kethuvim (writings) -- hence acronym: TNK- TaNaKh. Referred to by Christians as "Old Testament" though the book ordering differs from the Christian Bible.
Tanakh (also Tanach) - the Hebrew Scriptures The term Tanakh is derived from initial letters of the three sections of the Hebrew Scriptures - Torah, Neviim and .

Tashlisch Means 'casting away' and refers to a tradition on Rosh Hashana of casting bread into a body of moving water to symbolize sins being removed.

Techelet/T'chelet/Tekhelet The blue cord on each corner of the tzitzit, "Bid them that they make them throughout their generations fringes in the corners of their garments, and that they put with the fringe of each corner a thread of blue." Numbers 15:38 Traditional Judaism doesn't add the blue cord to their tzitzit, arguing they aren't sure about identifying the chilazon, a snail of Tyre from which the Phoenicians traditionally extracted the blue dye. Second century sages felt this was too expensive a dye to use, so they waived the biblical requirement, lest people use a cheaper dye instead and break the oral law. Written Torah never commanded the blue dye come from this particular snail, in fact, any blue dye would fulfill this command.

Tefillah Means 'prayer'

Tefillin Means 'remembrance' - these are leather boxes containing scrolls with Scripture passages, the rabbis interpreted literally G-d's command to wear His Word on hands and forehead -- for more info, see Mezuzah.

Teshuvah Means 'return' as in 'return to G-d; teshuvah is the way to repent: to stop and turn in the direction of G-d.

Tikkun Olam Refers to 'repairing the world' through mitzvah -- a noble concept but ignores the fact we need Messiah to return to set things right -- repairing the world isn't man's 'do it yourself' project.

Tisha B'Av Means the 'ninth of Av' -- a fast day remembering the temple destructions.

Torah Means 'instruction' and refers to the books of Moshe -- the 'law' comprised of the books: Genesis, Exodus, Leviticus, Numbers, and

Deuteronomy. 'Torah' is also used loosely in traditional Judaism to mean all Jewish law, Scriptural and oral. It can also be used to mean the Ten Commandments

Torah - A term used with various meanings. The fact it has so many uses makes it easy for some to conceal flawed logic. Commonly it is used to refer to the first five books of the Tanakh, either with or without the addition of the "Oral Torah". It may also, more narrowly, be used to refer to the Ten Commandments.

Tractate
A section or book from Mishneh and Talmud.

Treyf/Treif Means 'torn' and refers to non-kosher meat, meats not sanctioned by G-d.

Tu B'Shevat New year for trees, an Israeli-style Arbor day celebrated by planting trees on the 15th of Shevat.

Tzaddik Means a 'righteous person.'

Tzedakah From same root as Tzaddik, meaning righteous, but refers to charity. Many Jewish homes have a small box for collecting money that will later be donated to a charitable cause.

Tzitzit Fringes G-d commanded be attached to the corners of men's garments.

U

Ushpitzin A rabbinic concept of inviting ancesters to one's sukkah (like Abraham, Isaac, Jacob, Joseph, Moses, Aaron and David).

V

Vayikra - the transliteration into English of the third book of the Tanakh (Hebrew Scriptures), also often commonly called Leviticus.

W

Western Wall The remaining portion of the old temple on the temple mount, also called the 'wailing wall.'

World to Come Olam Haba -- the coming messianic kingdom when there will be peace on earth.

X

Xianity - a term used in place of Christianity by religious Jews to avoid the use of the word Christ even in a compound noun.

Y

Yad A hand-shaped pointer used when reading from Torah.

Yahrzeit Means 'anniversary' -- marking the anniversary of a deceased family member.

Yarmulke Aka kippah -- this is the skullcap worn by Jews, the cap is a fairly recent non-Scriptural tradition.

Yahveh - the God who met with Moshe (Moses) at Sinai. Contrary to modern custom the Hebrew text of the Tanakh makes it clear that God was referred to as Yahveh both in speech and in prayer.

Yechezkiel - a transliteration of the Hebrew name of the Tanakh prophet often referred to as Ezekiel.

Yehud/Yehudi Jew and Jews

Yerushalayim/Yerushalom Jerusalem

Yeshiva Talmudic and Torah academy

Yeshiva Bocher Unmarried male student student at Yeshiva

Yeshua Means 'Salvation' and is the real name of 'Jesus' in Hebrew. "And she shall bring forth a son, and thou shalt call his name Yeshua: for he shall save his people from their sins." Matthew 1:21 Transliterated into greek it would be derived in to english as "Jesus." The reason Messianic Jews use Yeshua instead of Jesus, is because Yeshua is His Name, and because Jewish people have been persecuted in the Name of Jesus. Yeshua communicates that our Messiah is for Jewish people, and not just for non-Jews.

Yetzer Ra In traditional Judaism, this means the 'evil impulse' which leads us to sin if not controlled.

Yetzer Tov In traditional Judaism, this means the 'good impulse' which leads us to obey G-d

Yiddish Originating among Ashkenazic Jews, this language is based on German using Hebrew letters.

Yisrael/Yisroel Israel

Yitzak - son of Avraham (Abraham). He is often referred to as Isaac.

Yom HaAtzmaut modern Israel's Independence Day

Yom HaShoah Holocaust Remembrance Day.

Yom HaZikaron modern Israel's Memorial Day

Yom Kippur Day of Atonement, holy day occuring ten days after Rosh Hoshana (Blowing of Trumpets). "It shall be an holy convocation unto you; and ye shall afflict your souls, and offer an offering made by fire unto YHVH." Leviticus 23:27 "Soul affliction" is interpreted by many to mean fasting.

Yom Yerushalayim Celebrates the 1967 recapture of Jerusalem.

Z

Zealots Revolutionary Judaism sect existing during time of Roman occupation in Israel around 1st and 2nd century BC, sect still popular at time of Yeshua.

Zohar Most likely written by Spanish kabbalist named Moses de Leon in the thirteenth century, some believe de Leon was merely redistributing a text originally written in the 1st century by Rabbi Shimon Bar Yokhai. Kabbalists tend to early-date the Zohar, others tend to late-date it.

XXIX 613 Mitzvot[14]

At the heart of halakhah is the unchangeable 613 mitzvot that G-d gave to the Jewish people in the Torah (the first five books of the Bible). The word "mitzvah" means "commandment." In its strictest sense, it refers only to commandments instituted in the Torah; however, the word is commonly used in a more generic sense to include all of the laws, practices and customs of halakhah, and is often used in an even more loose way to refer to any good deed.

Some of the mitzvot are clear, explicit commands in the Bible (thou shalt not murder; to write words of Torah on the doorposts of your house), others are more implicit (the mitzvah to recite grace after meals, which is inferred from "and you will eat and be satisfied and bless the L-rd your G-d"), and some can only be ascertained by Talmudic logic (that a man shall not commit incest with his daughter, which is derived from the commandment not to commit incest with his daughter's daughter).

Some of the mitzvot overlap; for example, it is a positive commandment to rest on the Sabbath and a negative commandment not to do work on the Sabbath.

Although there is not 100% agreement on the precise list of the 613 (there are some slight discrepancies in the way some lists divide related or overlapping mitzvot), there is complete agreement that there are 613 mitzvot. This number is significant: it is the numeric value of the word Torah (Tav = 400, Vav = 6, Resh = 200, Heh = 5), plus 2 for the two mitzvot whose existence precedes the Torah: I am the L-rd, your G-d and You shall have no other gods before Me. There is also complete agreement that these 613 mitzvot can be broken down into 248 positive mitzvot (one for each bone and organ of the male body) and 365 negative mitzvot (one for each day of the solar year).

---

[14] Jewish Virtual Library

The most accepted list of the 613 mitzvot is Maimonides' list in his Mishneh Torah. In the introduction to the first book of the Mishneh Torah, Maimonides lists all of the positive mitzvot and all of the negative mitzvot, then proceeds to divide them up into subject matter categories. See List of the 613 Mitzvot.

Many of these 613 mitzvot cannot be observed at this time for various reasons. For example, a large portion of the laws relate to sacrifices and offerings, which can only be made in the Temple, and the Temple does not exist today. Some of the laws relate to the theocratic state of Israel, its king, its supreme court, and its system of justice, and cannot be observed because the theocratic state of Israel does not exist today. In addition, some laws do not apply to all people or places. Agricultural laws only apply within the state of Israel, and certain laws only apply to kohanim or Levites. The modern scholar Rabbi Israel Meir of Radin, commonly known as the Chafetz Chayim, has identified 77 positive mitzvot and 194 negative mitzvot which can be observed outside of Israel today.

All 613 Commandments in the Torah

There are a whole lot more than only 10 Commandments found in the Old Testament, there are 613 Commandments! Below is a list of the 613 mitzvot commandments (mitzvot is plural, mitzvah is singular).

There are both "positive" and "negative" mitzvot (do's and don'ts) which can be divided into 365 Negative Mitzvot (to remind us not to do bad things every day of the year) plus 248 Positive Mitzvot (the number of bones in the human body - for a total of 613. In this way, Hebrews and Jewish people are able to obey the mitzvot with their entire body.

It is important to know that while God gave us many commands to follow, including the famous Ten Commandments, He did not abolish the Law of Moses found in the Torah (the first five Books of the Bible). The following commandments are superceded by the new covenant of grace.

The Law is God's Divine Instructions in Righteousness without which man would have NO blueprint for moral, holy living.

Yeshua only was against rabbinical, man-made opinions and traditions that kept people in bondage. Neither He nor His apostles ever spoke against the Law nor suggested that after Jesus' death the Torah was to become null and void.

The Apostle Paul said, *"Do we then nullify the Law through faith? May it never be! On the contrary, we establish the Law."* (Romans 3:31)

God gave 248 positive Mitzvot / Commandments ("the Do's"), and 365 negative ones ("the Don'ts"). They are as follows:

The 248 Positive Mitzvot / Commandments: "The Do's"

RELATIONSHIP TO GOD

1 Exodus 20:2 - **To believe in God.**
I am the Lord thy God, which have brought thee out of the land of Egypt, out of the house of bondage.
2 Deuteronomy 6:4 - **To acknowledge the Unity of God.**
Hear, O Israel: The Lord our God is one Lord:
3 Deuteronomy 6:5 - **To love God.**
And thou shalt love the Lord thy God with all thine heart, and with all thy soul, and with all thy might.
4 Deuteronomy 6:13 - **To fear God.**
Thou shalt fear the Lord thy God, and serve him, and shalt swear by his name.
5 Exodus 23:25; Deuteronomy 11:13; 13:4 - **To serve God.**
And ye shall serve the Lord your God, and he shall bless thy bread, and thy water; and I will take sickness away from the midst of thee.
6 Deuteronomy 10:20 - **To cleave to God.**
Thou shalt fear the Lord thy God; him shalt thou serve, and to him shalt thou cleave, and swear by his name.
7 Deuteronomy 10:20 - **On taking an oath by God's Name.**
Thou shalt fear the Lord thy God; him shalt thou serve, and to him shalt thou cleave, and swear by his name.
8 Deuteronomy 28:9 - **On walking in God's ways.**
The Lord shall establish thee an holy people unto himself, as he

hath sworn unto thee, if thou shalt keep the commandments of the Lord thy God, and walk in his ways.

9 Leviticus 22:32 - **On Sanctifying God's Name.**
Neither shall ye profane my holy name; but I will be hallowed among the children of Israel: I am the Lord which hallow you,

TORAH

10 Deuteronomy 6:7 - **On reciting the Sh'ma each morning and evening.**
And thou shalt teach them diligently unto thy children, and shalt talk of them when thou sittest in thine house, and when thou walkest by the way, and when thou liest down, and when thou risest up.

11 Deuteronomy 6:7 - **On studying and teaching Torah.**
And thou shalt teach them diligently unto thy children, and shalt talk of them when thou sittest in thine house, and when thou walkest by the way, and when thou liest down, and when thou risest up.

12 Deuteronomy 6:8 - **On binding Tefillin on the head.**
And thou shalt bind them for a sign upon thine hand, and they shall be as frontlets between thine eyes.

13 Deuteronomy 6:8 - **On binding Tefillin on the hand.**
And thou shalt bind them for a sign upon thine hand, and they shall be as frontlets between thine eyes.

14 Numbers 15:38 - **On making Tzitzit with thread of blue, garments corners.**
Speak unto the children of Israel, and bid them that they make them fringes in the borders of their garments throughout their generations, and that they put upon the fringe of the borders a ribband of blue:

15 Deuteronomy 6:9 - **On affixing a Mezuzah to doorposts and gates.**
And thou shalt write them upon the posts of thy house, and on thy gates.

16 Deuteronomy 31:12 - **On Assembling each 7th year to hear the Torah read.**
Gather the people together, men, and women, and children, and thy stranger that is within thy gates, that they may hear, and that they may learn, and fear the Lord your God, and observe to do all the words of this law:

17 Deuteronomy 17:18 - **On that a king must write a copy of Torah for himself.**
And it shall be, when he sitteth upon the throne of his kingdom, that he shall write him a copy of this law in a book out of that which is before the priests the Levites:

18 Deuteronomy 31:19 - **On that everyone should have a Torah scroll.**
Now therefore write ye this song for you, and teach it the children of Israel: put it in their mouths, that this song may be a witness for me against the children of Israel.

19 Deuteronomy 8:10 - **On praising God after eating, Grace after meals.**
When thou hast eaten and art full, then thou shalt bless the Lord thy God for the good land which he hath given thee.

TEMPLE AND THE PRIESTS

20 Exodus 25:8 - **On building a Sanctuary / (Tabernacle / Temple) for God.**
And let them make me a sanctuary; that I may dwell among

them.

21 *Leviticus 19:30 -* **On respecting the Sanctuary.**

Ye shall keep my sabbaths, and reverence my sanctuary: I am the Lord.

22 *Numbers 18:4 -* **On guarding the Sanctuary.**

And they shall be joined unto thee, and keep the charge of the tabernacle of the congregation, for all the service of the tabernacle: and a stranger shall not come nigh unto you.

23 *Numbers 18:23 -* **On Levitical services in the Tabernacle.**

But the Levites shall do the service of the tabernacle of the congregation, and they shall bear their iniquity: it shall be a statute for ever throughout your generations, that among the children of Israel they have no inheritance.

24 *Exodus 30:19 -* **On Cohanim (Priests) washing hands and feet before entering Temple.**

For Aaron and his sons shall wash their hands and their feet thereat;

25 *Exodus 27:21 -* **On kindling the Menorah by the Cohanim (Priests).**

In the tabernacle of the congregation without the vail, which is before the testimony, Aaron and his sons shall order it from evening to morning before the Lord: it shall be a statute for ever unto their generations on the behalf of the children of Israel.

26 *Numbers 6:23 -* **On the Cohanim (Priests) blessing Israel.**

Speak unto Aaron and unto his sons, saying, On this wise ye shall bless the children of Israel, saying unto them,

27 *Exodus 25:30 -* **On the Showbread before the Ark.**

And thou shalt set upon the table shewbread before me alway.

28 *Exodus 30:7 -* **On Burning the Incense on the Golden Altar twice daily.**

And Aaron shall burn thereon sweet incense every morning: when he dresseth the lamps, he shall burn incense upon it.

29 *Leviticus 6:13 -* **On the perpetual fire on the Altar.**
The fire shall ever be burning upon the altar; it shall never go out.

30 *Leviticus 6:10 -* **On removing the ashes from the Altar.**
And the priest shall put on his linen garment, and his linen breeches shall he put upon his flesh, and take up the ashes which the fire hath consumed with the burnt offering on the altar, and he shall put them beside the altar.

31 *Numbers 5:2 -* **On removing unclean persons from the camp.**
Command the children of Israel, that they put out of the camp every leper, and every one that hath an issue, and whosoever is defiled by the dead:

32 *Leviticus 21:8 -* **On honoring the Cohanim (Priests).**
Thou shalt sanctify him therefore; for he offereth the bread of thy God: he shall be holy unto thee: for I the Lord, which sanctify you, am holy.

33 *Exodus 28:2 -* **On the garments of the Cohanim (Priests).**
And thou shalt make holy garments for Aaron thy brother for glory and for beauty.

34 *Numbers 7:9 -* **On Cohanim (Priests) bearing the Ark on their shoulders.**
But unto the sons of Kohath he gave none: because the service of the sanctuary belonging unto them was that they should bear upon their shoulders.

35 *Exodus 30:31 -* **On the holy anointing oil.**
And thou shalt speak unto the children of Israel, saying, This shall be an holy anointing oil unto me throughout your generations.

36 *Deuteronomy 18:6-8 -* **On the Cohanim (Priests) ministering in rotation / watches.**

And if a Levite come from any of thy gates out of all Israel, where he sojourned, and come with all the desire of his mind unto the place which the Lord shall choose; Then he shall minister in the name of the Lord his God, as all his brethren the Levites do, which stand there before the Lord. They shall have like portions to eat, beside that which cometh of the sale of his patrimony.

37 *Leviticus 21:2-3 -* **On the Cohanim (Priests) being defiled for dead relatives.**

But for his kin, that is near unto him, that is, for his mother, and for his father, and for his son, and for his daughter, and for his brother. And for his sister a virgin, that is nigh unto him, which hath had no husband; for her may he be defiled.

38 *Leviticus 21:13 -* **On that Cohen haGadol (High Priest) may only marry a virgin.**

And he shall take a wife in her virginity.

SACRIFICES

39 *Numbers 28:3 -* **On the twice Daily Burnt, tamid, offerings.**
And thou shalt say unto them, This is the offering made by fire which ye shall offer unto the Lord; two lambs of the first year without spot day by day, for a continual burnt offering.

40 *Leviticus 6:20 -* **On Cohen haGadol's (High Priest) twice daily meal offering.**

This is the offering of Aaron and of his sons, which they shall offer unto the Lord in the day when he is anointed; the tenth part of an ephah of fine flour for a meat offering perpetual, half of it in the morning, and half thereof at night.

41 *Numbers 28:9 -* **On the Shabbat additional, musaf, offering.**

And on the sabbath day two lambs of the first year without spot, and two tenth deals of flour for a meat offering, mingled with oil, and the drink offering thereof:

42 *Numbers 28:11 -* **On the New Moon, Rosh Chodesh, additional offering.**

And in the beginnings of your months ye shall offer a burnt offering unto the Lord; two young bullocks, and one ram, seven lambs of the first year without spot;

43 *Leviticus 23:36 -* **On Pesach (Passover) additional offering.**

Seven days ye shall offer an offering made by fire unto the Lord: on the eighth day shall be an holy convocation unto you; and ye shall offer an offering made by fire unto the Lord: it is a solemn assembly; and ye shall do no servile work therein.

44 *Leviticus 23:15 -* **On the second day of Pesach (Passover) meal offering of the Omer (Counting).**

And ye shall count unto you from the morrow after the sabbath, from the day that ye brought the sheaf of the wave offering; seven sabbaths shall be complete:

45 *Numbers 28:26 -* **On Shavuot (Pentecost) additional, musaf, offering.**

Also in the day of the firstfruits, when ye bring a new meat offering unto the Lord, after your weeks be out, ye shall have a holy convocation; ye shall do no servile work:

46 *Leviticus 23:17 -* **On the Two Loaves of bread Wave offering on Shavuot (Pentecost).**

Ye shall bring out of your habitations two wave loaves of two tenth deals: they shall be of fine flour; they shall be baken with leaven; they are the firstfruits unto the Lord

47 *Numbers 29:1-2 -* **On Rosh HaShannah (Head of Year) additional offering.**

And in the seventh month, on the first day of the month, ye shall have an holy convocation; ye shall do no servile work: it is a day of blowing the trumpets unto you. And ye shall offer a burnt offering for a sweet savour unto the Lord; one young bullock, one ram, and seven lambs of the first year without blemish:

48 *Numbers 29:7-8 -* **On Yom Kippur (Day of Atonement) additional offering.**

And ye shall have on the tenth day of this seventh month an holy convocation; and ye shall afflict your souls: ye shall not do any work therein: But ye shall offer a burnt offering unto the Lord for a sweet savour; one young bullock, one ram, and seven lambs of the first year; they shall be unto you without blemish:

49 *Leviticus 16 -* **On the service of Yom Kippur, Avodah.**

And this shall be a statute for ever unto you: that in the seventh month, on the tenth day of the month, ye shall afflict your souls, and do no work at all, whether it be one of your own country, or a stranger that sojourneth among you: For on that day shall the priest make an atonement for you, to cleanse you, that ye may be clean from all your sins before the Lord. It shall be a sabbath of rest unto you, and ye shall afflict your souls, by a statute for ever.

50 *Numbers 29:13 -* **On Sukkot, musaf, offerings.**

And ye shall offer a burnt offering, a sacrifice made by fire, of a sweet savour unto the Lord; thirteen young bullocks, two rams, and fourteen lambs of the first year; they shall be without blemish:

51 *Numbers 29:36 -* **On the Shemini Atzeret additional offering.**

But ye shall offer a burnt offering, a sacrifice made by fire, of a sweet savour unto the Lord: one bullock, one ram, seven lambs of the first year without blemish:

52 *Exodus 23:14 -* **On the three annual Festival pilgrimages to the Temple.**

Three times thou shalt keep a feast unto me in the year.

53 *Exodus 34:23 -* **On appearing before YHVH during the**

Festivals.

Thrice in the year shall all your men children appear before the LORD GOD, the God of Israel.

54 *Deuteronomy 16:14 - **On rejoicing on the Festivals.***

And thou shalt rejoice in thy feast, thou, and thy son, and thy daughter, and thy manservant, and thy maidservant, and the Levite, the stranger, and the fatherless, and the widow, that are within thy gates.

55 *Exodus 12:6 - **On the 14th of Nisan slaughtering the Pesach (Passover) lamb.***

And ye shall keep it up until the fourteenth day of the same month: and the whole assembly of the congregation of Israel shall kill it in the evening.

56 *Exodus 12:8 - **On eating the roasted Pesach (Passover) lamb night of Nisan 15th.***

And they shall eat the flesh in that night, roast with fire, and unleavened bread; and with bitter herbs they shall eat it.

57 *Numbers 9:11 - **On slaughtering the Pesach (Passover) Sheini, Iyyar 14th, offering.***

The fourteenth day of the second month at even they shall keep it, and eat it with unleavened bread and bitter herbs.

58 *Numbers 9:11 - **On eating the Pesach (Passover) Sheini lamb with Matzah and Maror.***

The fourteenth day of the second month at even they shall keep it, and eat it with unleavened bread and bitter herbs.

59 *Numbers 10:9-10 - **Trumpets for Feast sacrifices brought and for tribulation.***

And if ye go to war in your land against the enemy that oppresseth you, then ye shall blow an alarm with the trumpets; and ye shall be remembered before the Lord your God, and ye shall be saved from your enemies. Also in the day of your gladness, and in your solemn days, and in the beginnings of your months, ye shall blow with the trumpets over your burnt offerings, and over the sacrifices of your peace offerings; that they may be to you for a memorial before your God: I am the Lord your God.

60 *Leviticus 22:27 -* **On minimum age of cattle to be offered.**
When a bullock, or a sheep, or a goat, is brought forth, then it shall be seven days under the dam; and from the eighth day and thenceforth it shall be accepted for an offering made by fire unto the Lord.

61 *Leviticus 22:21 -* **On offering only unblemished sacrifices.**
And whosoever offereth a sacrifice of peace offerings unto the Lord to accomplish his vow, or a freewill offering in beeves or sheep, it shall be perfect to be accepted; there shall be no blemish therein.

62 *Leviticus 2:13 -* **On bringing salt with every offering.**
And every oblation of thy meat offering shalt thou season with salt; neither shalt thou suffer the salt of the covenant of thy God to be lacking from thy meat offering: with all thine offerings thou shalt offer salt.

63 *Leviticus 1:2 -* **On the Burnt-Offering.**
Speak unto the children of Israel, and say unto them, If any man of you bring an offering unto the Lord, ye shall bring your offering of the cattle, even of the herd, and of the flock.

64 *Leviticus 6:25 -* **On the Sin-Offering.**
Speak unto Aaron and to his sons, saying, This is the law of the sin offering: In the place where the burnt offering is killed shall the sin offering be killed before the Lord: it is most holy.

65 *Leviticus 7:1 -* **On the Guilt-Offering.**
Likewise this is the law of the trespass offering: it is most holy.

66 *Leviticus 3:1 -* **On the Peace-Offering.**
And if his oblation be a sacrifice of peace offering, if he offer it of

the herd; whether it be a male or female, he shall offer it without blemish before the Lord.

67 *Leviticus 2:1 -* **On the Meal-Offering.**

And when any will offer a meat offering unto the Lord, his offering shall be of fine flour; and he shall pour oil upon it, and put frankincense thereon:

68 *Leviticus 4:13 -* **On offerings for a Court (Sanhedrin) that has erred.**

And if the whole congregation of Israel sin through ignorance, and the thing be hid from the eyes of the assembly, and they have done somewhat against any of the commandments of the Lord concerning things which should not be done, and are guilty;

69 *Leviticus 4:27 -* **Fixed Sin-Offering, by one unknowingly breaking a commandment.**

And if any one of the common people sin through ignorance, while he doeth somewhat against any of the commandments of the Lord concerning things which ought not to be done, and be guilty;

70 *Leviticus 5:17 -* **Suspensive Guilt-Offering if doubt of breaking a commandment.**

And if a soul sin, and commit any of these things which are forbidden to be done by the commandments of the Lord; though he wist it not, yet is he guilty, and shall bear his iniquity.

71 *Leviticus 5:15 -* **Unconditional Guilt-Offering, for stealing, etc.**

If a soul commit a trespass, and sin through ignorance, in the holy things of the Lord; then he shall bring for his trespass unto the Lord a ram without blemish out of the flocks, with thy estimation by shekels of silver, after the shekel of the sanctuary, for a trespass offering:

72 *Leviticus 5:11 -* **Offering higher or lower value, according to**

ones means.

But if he be not able to bring two turtledoves, or two young pigeons, then he that sinned shall bring for his offering the tenth part of an ephah of fine flour for a sin offering; he shall put no oil upon it, neither shall he put any frankincense thereon: for it is a sin offering.

73 Numbers 5:6-7 - **To confess one's sins before God and repent from them.**

Speak unto the children of Israel, When a man or woman shall commit any sin that men commit, to do a trespass against the Lord, and that person be guilty; Then they shall confess their sin which they have done: and he shall recompense his trespass with the principal thereof, and add unto it the fifth part thereof, and give it unto him against whom he hath trespassed.

74 Leviticus 15:13 - **On offering brought by a zav (man with a discharge).**

And when he that hath an issue is cleansed of his issue; then he shall number to himself seven days for his cleansing, and wash his clothes, and bathe his flesh in running water, and shall be clean.

75 Leviticus 15:28 - **Offering brought by a zavah (woman with a discharge).**

But if she be cleansed of her issue, then she shall number to herself seven days, and after that she shall be clean.

76 Leviticus 12:6 - **On offering brought by a woman after childbirth.**

And when the days of her purifying are fulfilled, for a son, or for a daughter, she shall bring a lamb of the first year for a burnt offering, and a young pigeon, or a turtledove, for a sin offering, unto the door of the tabernacle of the congregation, unto the priest:

*77 Leviticus 14:10 - **On offering brought by a leper after being cleansed.***

And on the eighth day he shall take two he lambs without blemish, and one ewe lamb of the first year without blemish, and three tenth deals of fine flour for a meat offering, mingled with oil, and one log of oil.

*78 Leviticus 27:32 - **On the Tithe of one's cattle.***

And concerning the tithe of the herd, or of the flock, even of whatsoever passeth under the rod, the tenth shall be holy unto the Lord.

*79 Exodus 13:2 - **Sacrificing the First-born of clean (permitted) cattle.***

Sanctify unto me all the firstborn, whatsoever openeth the womb among the children of Israel, both of man and of beast: it is mine.

*80 Exodus 22:29 - **On Redeeming the First-born of man, Pidyon ha-ben.***

Thou shalt not delay to offer the first of thy ripe fruits, and of thy liquors: the firstborn of thy sons shalt thou give unto me.

*81 Exodus 34:20 - **On Redeeming the firstling of an ass, if not...***

But the firstling of an ass thou shalt redeem with a lamb: and if thou redeem him not, then shalt thou break his neck. All the firstborn of thy sons thou shalt redeem. And none shall appear before me empty.

*82 Exodus 13:13 - **...breaking the neck of the firstling of an ass.***

And every firstling of an ass thou shalt redeem with a lamb; and if thou wilt not redeem it, then thou shalt break his neck: and all the firstborn of man among thy children shalt thou redeem.

*83 Deuteronomy 12:5 - **On bringing due offerings to Jerusalem without delay.***

But unto the place which the Lord your God shall choose out of all your tribes to put his name there, even unto his habitation shall ye seek, and thither thou shalt come:

84 Deuteronomy 12:14 - **All offerings must be brought only to the Sanctuary.**

But in the place which the Lord shall choose in one of thy tribes, there thou shalt offer thy burnt offerings, and there thou shalt do all that I command thee.

85 Deuteronomy 12:26 - **On offerings due from outside Israel to the Sanctuary.**

Only thy holy things which thou hast, and thy vows, thou shalt take, and go unto the place which the Lord shall choose:

86 Deuteronomy 12:15 - **On Redeeming blemished sanctified animal offerings.**

Notwithstanding, thou mayest kill and eat flesh in all thy gates, whatsoever thy soul lusteth after, according to the blessing of the Lord thy God which he hath given thee: the unclean and the clean may eat thereof, as of the roebuck, and as of the hart.

87 Leviticus 27:33 - **On the holiness of substituted animal offerings.**

He shall not search whether it be good or bad, neither shall he change it: and if he change it at all, then both it and the change thereof shall be holy; it shall not be redeemed.

88 Leviticus 6:9 - **On Cohanim (Priests) eating the remainder of the Meal Offerings.**

Command Aaron and his sons, saying, This is the law of the burnt offering: It is the burnt offering, because of the burning upon the altar all night unto the morning, and the fire of the altar shall be burning in it.

89 Exodus 29:33 - **On Cohanim (Priests) eating the meat of Sin and Guilt Offerings.**

And they shall eat those things wherewith the atonement was

*made, to consecrate and to sanctify them: but a stranger shall not
eat thereof, because they are holy.*

90 *Leviticus 7:19 -* **Burn Consecrated Offerings that've
become tameh/unclean.**
*And the flesh that toucheth any unclean thing shall not be eaten;
it shall be burnt with fire: and as for the flesh, all that be clean
shall eat thereof.*

91 *Leviticus 7:17 -* **Burn remnant of Consecrated Offerings not
eaten in time.**
*But the remainder of the flesh of the sacrifice on the third day
shall be burnt with fire.*

VOWS

92 *Numbers 6:5 -* **The Nazirite letting his hair grow during his
separation.**
*All the days of the vow of his separation there shall no razor
come upon his head: until the days be fulfilled, in the which he
separateth himself unto the Lord, he shall be holy, and shall let
the locks of the hair of his head grow.*

93 *Numbers 6:18 –* **Nazirite completing vow shaves his head and
brings sacrifice.**
*And the Nazarite shall shave the head of his separation at the
door of the tabernacle of the congregation, and shall take the
hair of the head of his separation, and put it in the fire which is
under the sacrifice of the peace offerings.*

94 *Deuteronomy 23:21 -* **On that a man must honor his oral
vows and oaths.**
*When thou shalt vow a vow unto the Lord thy God, thou shalt not
slack to pay it: for the Lord thy God will surely require it of thee;
and it would be sin in thee.*

95 *Numbers 30:8 -* **On that a judge can annul vows, only according to Torah.**
But if her husband disallowed her on the day that he heard it; then he shall make her vow which she vowed, and that which she uttered with her lips, wherewith she bound her soul, of none effect: and the Lord shall forgive her.

RITUAL PURITY

96 *Leviticus 11:8 -* **Defilement by touching certain animal carcasses, and...**
Of their flesh shall ye not eat, and their carcase shall ye not touch; they are unclean to you.
97 *Leviticus 11:29 -* **...by touching carcasses of eight creeping creatures.**
These also shall be unclean unto you among the creeping things that creep upon the earth; the weasel, and the mouse, and the tortoise after his kind,
98 *Leviticus 11:34 -* **Defilement of food and drink, if contacting unclean thing.**
Of all meat which may be eaten, that on which such water cometh shall be unclean: and all drink that may be drunk in every such vessel shall be unclean.
99 *Leviticus 15:19 -* **On Tumah (unclean) of a menstruant woman.**
And if a woman have an issue, and her issue in her flesh be blood, she shall be put apart seven days: and whosoever toucheth her shall be unclean until the even.
100 *Leviticus 12:2 -* **On Tumah (unclean) of a woman after childbirth.**
Speak unto the children of Israel, saying, If a woman have

conceived seed, and born a man child, then she shall be unclean seven days; according to the days of the separation for her infirmity shall she be unclean.

101 *Leviticus 13:3 -* **On Tumah (unclean) of a leper.**
And the priest shall look on the plague in the skin of the flesh: and when the hair in the plague is turned white, and the plague in sight be deeper than the skin of his flesh, it is a plague of leprosy: and the priest shall look on him, and pronounce him unclean.

102 *Leviticus 13:51 -* **On garments contaminated by leprosy.**
And he shall look on the plague on the seventh day: if the plague be spread in the garment, either in the warp, or in the woof, or in a skin, or in any work that is made of skin; the plague is a fretting leprosy; it is unclean.

103 *Leviticus 14:44 -* **On a leprous house.**
Then the priest shall come and look, and, behold, if the plague be spread in the house, it is a fretting leprosy in the house: it is unclean.

104 *Leviticus 15:2 -* **On Tumah (unclean) of a zav (man with a running issue).**
Speak unto the children of Israel, and say unto them, When any man hath a running issue out of his flesh, because of his issue he is unclean.

105 *Leviticus 15:6 -* **On Tumah (unclean) of semen.**
And he that sitteth on any thing whereon he sat that hath the issue shall wash his clothes, and bathe himself in water, and be unclean until the even.

106 *Leviticus 15:19 -* **Tumah (unclean) of a zavah (woman suffering from a running issue).**
And if a woman have an issue, and her issue in her flesh be blood, she shall be put apart seven days: and whosoever toucheth her shall be unclean until the even.

107 Numbers 19:14 - **On Tumah (unclean) of a human corpse.**
This is the law, when a man dieth in a tent: all that come into the tent, and all that is in the tent, shall be unclean seven days.
108 Numbers 19:13 - **Law of the purification water of sprinkling, mei niddah.**
Whosoever toucheth the dead body of any man that is dead, and purifieth not himself, defileth the tabernacle of the Lord; and that soul shall be cut off from Israel: because the water of separation was not sprinkled upon him, he shall be unclean; his uncleanness is yet upon him.
109 Leviticus 15:16 - **On immersing in a mikveh to become ritually clean.**
And if any mans seed of copulation go out from him, then he shall wash all his flesh in water, and be unclean until the even.
110 Leviticus 14:2 - **On the specified procedure of cleansing from leprosy.**
This shall be the law of the leper in the day of his cleansing: He shall be brought unto the priest:
111 Leviticus 14:9 - **On that a leper must shave his head.**
But it shall be on the seventh day, that he shall shave all his hair off his head and his beard and his eyebrows, even all his hair he shall shave off: and he shall wash his clothes, also he shall wash his flesh in water, and he shall be clean.
112 Leviticus 13:45 - **On that the leper must be made easily distinguishable.**
And the leper in whom the plague is, his clothes shall be rent, and his head bare, and he shall put a covering upon his upper lip, and shall cry, Unclean, unclean.
113 Numbers 19:2 - **On Ashes of the Red Heifer, used in ritual purification.**
This is the ordinance of the law which the Lord hath commanded,

saying, Speak unto the children of Israel, that they bring thee a red heifer without spot, wherein is no blemish, and upon which never came yoke:

DONATIONS TO THE TEMPLE

114 *Leviticus 27:2 -* **On the valuation for a person himself to the Temple.**
Speak unto the children of Israel, and say unto them, When a man shall make a singular vow, the persons shall be for the Lord by thy estimation.
115 *Leviticus 27:11 -* **On the valuation for an unclean beast to the Temple.**
And if it be any unclean beast, of which they do not offer a sacrifice unto the Lord, then he shall present the beast before the priest:
116 *Leviticus 27:14 -* **On the valuation of a house as a donation to the Temple.**
And when a man shall sanctify his house to be holy unto the Lord, then the priest shall estimate it, whether it be good or bad: as the priest shall estimate it, so shall it stand.
117 *Leviticus 27:16 -* **On the valuation of a field as a donation to the Temple.**
And if a man shall sanctify unto the Lord some part of a field of his possession, then thy estimation shall be according to the seed thereof: an homer of barley seed shall be valued at fifty shekels of silver.
118 *Leviticus 5:16 -* **If benefit from Temple property, restitution plus 1/5th.**
And he shall make amends for the harm that he hath done in the holy thing, and shall add the fifth part thereto, and give it unto

the priest: and the priest shall make an atonement for him with the ram of the trespass offering, and it shall be forgiven him.

119 Leviticus 19:24 - **On the fruits of the trees fourth year's growth.**

But in the fourth year all the fruit thereof shall be holy to praise the Lord withal.

120 Leviticus 19:9 - **On leaving the corners (Peah) of fields for the poor.**

And when ye reap the harvest of your land, thou shalt not wholly reap the corners of thy field, neither shalt thou gather the gleanings of thy harvest.

121 Leviticus 19:9 - **On leaving gleanings of the field for the poor.**

And when ye reap the harvest of your land, thou shalt not wholly reap the corners of thy field, neither shalt thou gather the gleanings of thy harvest.

122 Deuteronomy 24:19 - **On leaving the forgotten sheaf for the poor.**

When thou cuttest down thine harvest in thy field, and hast forgot a sheaf in the field, thou shalt not go again to fetch it: it shall be for the stranger, for the fatherless, and for the widow: that the Lord thy God may bless thee in all the work of thine hands.

123 Leviticus 19:10 - **On leaving the misformed grape clusters for the poor.**

And thou shalt not glean thy vineyard, neither shalt thou gather every grape of thy vineyard; thou shalt leave them for the poor and stranger: I am the Lord your God.

124 Leviticus 19:10 - **On leaving grape gleanings for the poor.**

And thou shalt not glean thy vineyard, neither shalt thou gather every grape of thy vineyard; thou shalt leave them for the poor and stranger: I am the Lord your God.

125 *Exodus 23:19 -* ***On separating and bringing First-fruits to the Sanctuary.***

The first of the firstfruits of thy land thou shalt bring into the house of the Lord thy God. Thou shalt not seethe a kid in his mothers milk.

126 *Deuteronomy 18:4 -* ***To separate the great Heave-offering (terumah).***

The firstfruit also of thy corn, of thy wine, and of thine oil, and the first of the fleece of thy sheep, shalt thou give him.

127 *Deuteronomy 14:29 -* ***To set aside the first tithe to the Levites.***

And the Levite, (because he hath no part nor inheritance with thee,) and the stranger, and the fatherless, and the widow, which are within thy gates, shall come, and shall eat and be satisfied; that the Lord thy God may bless thee in all the work of thine hand which thou doest.

128 *Deuteronomy 14:22 -* ***To set aside the second tithe, eaten only in Jerusalem.***

Thou shalt truly tithe all the increase of thy seed, that the field bringeth forth year by year.

129 *Numbers 18:26 -* ***On Levites' giving tenth of their tithe to the Cohanim (High Priests).***

Thus speak unto the Levites, and say unto them, When ye take of the children of Israel the tithes which I have given you from them for your inheritance, then ye shall offer up an heave offering of it for the Lord, even a tenth part of the tithe.

130 *Deuteronomy 14:28 -* ***To set aside the poor-man's tithe in 3rd and 6th year.***

At the end of three years thou shalt bring forth all the tithe of thine increase the same year, and shalt lay it up within thy gates:

131 *Deuteronomy 26:13 -* ***A declaration made when separating***

the various tithes.

Then thou shalt say before the Lord thy God, I have brought away the hallowed things out of mine house, and also have given them unto the Levite, and unto the stranger, to the fatherless, and to the widow, according to all thy commandments which thou hast commanded me: I have not transgressed thy commandments, neither have I forgotten them:

132 *Deuteronomy 26:2 -* ***A declaration made bringing First-fruits to the Temple.***

That thou shalt take of the first of all the fruit of the earth, which thou shalt bring of thy land that the Lord thy God giveth thee, and shalt put it in a basket, and shalt go unto the place which the Lord thy God shall choose to place his name there.

133 *Numbers 15:20 -* ***On the first portion of the Challah given to the Cohen (Priest).***

Ye shall offer up a cake of the first of your dough for an heave offering: as ye do the heave offering of the threshingfloor, so shall ye heave it.

THE SABBATICAL YEAR

134 *Exodus 23:11 -* ***On ownerless produce of the Sabbatical year (shemittah) .***

But the seventh year thou shalt let it rest and lie still; that the poor of thy people may eat: and what they leave the beasts of the field shall eat. In like manner thou shalt deal with thy vineyard, and with thy oliveyard.

135 *Leviticus 25:4 -* ***On resting the land on the Sabbatical year.***

But in the seventh year shall be a sabbath of rest unto the land, a sabbath for the LORD: thou shalt neither sow thy field, nor prune thy vineyard.

136 Leviticus 25:10 - **On sanctifying the Jubilee (50th) year.**
And ye shall hallow the fiftieth year, and proclaim liberty throughout all the land unto all the inhabitants thereof: it shall be a jubile unto you; and ye shall return every man unto his possession, and ye shall return every man unto his family.

137 Leviticus 25:9 - **Blow Shofar on Yom Kippur (Day of Atonement) in the Jubilee and slaves freed.**
Then shalt thou cause the trumpet of the jubile to sound on the tenth day of the seventh month, in the day of atonement shall ye make the trumpet sound throughout all your land.

138 Leviticus 25:25 - **Reversion of the land to ancestral owners in Jubilee year.**
If thy brother be waxen poor, and hath sold away some of his possession, and if any of his kin come to redeem it, then shall he redeem that which his brother sold.

139 Leviticus 25:24 - **On the redemption of a house within a year of the sale.**
And in all the land of your possession ye shall grant a redemption for the land.

140 Leviticus 25:8 - **Counting and announcing the years till the Jubilee year.**
And thou shalt number seven sabbaths of years unto thee, seven times seven years; and the space of the seven sabbaths of years shall be unto thee forty and nine years.

141 Deuteronomy 15:3 - **All debts are annulled in the Sabbatical year, but...**
Of a foreigner thou mayest exact it again: but that which is thine with thy brother thine hand shall release;

142 Deuteronomy 15:3 - **...one may exact a debt owed by a foreigner.**
Of a foreigner thou mayest exact it again: but that which is thine

with thy brother thine hand shall release;

CONCERNING ANIMALS FOR CONSUMPTION

143 Deuteronomy 18:3 - **The Cohen's (Priest's) due in the slaughter of every clean animal.**
And this shall be the priest's due from the people, from them that offer a sacrifice, whether it be ox or sheep; and they shall give unto the priest the shoulder, and the two cheeks, and the maw.
144 Deuteronomy 18:4 - **On the first of the fleece to be given to the Cohen (Priest).**
The firstfruit also of thy corn, of thy wine, and of thine oil, and the first of the fleece of thy sheep, shalt thou give him.
145 Leviticus 27:21 - **(Cherem vow) one devoted thing to God, other to Cohanim (Priest).**
But the field, when it goeth out in the jubile, shall be holy unto the LORD, as a field devoted; the possession thereof shall be the priest's.
146 Deuteronomy 12:21 - **Slaughtering animals, according to Torah, before eating.**
If the place which the LORD thy God hath chosen to put his name there be too far from thee, then thou shalt kill of thy herd and of thy flock, which the LORD hath given thee, as I have commanded thee, and thou shalt eat in thy gates whatsoever thy soul lusteth after.
147 Leviticus 17:13 - **Covering with earth the blood of slain fowl and beast.**
And whatsoever man there be of the children of Israel, or of the strangers that sojourn among you, which hunteth and catcheth any beast or fowl that may be eaten; he shall even pour out the blood thereof, and cover it with dust.

148 *Deuteronomy 22:7 -* **On setting free the parent bird when taking the nest.**
But thou shalt in any wise let the dam go, and take the young to thee; that it may be well with thee, and that thou mayest prolong thy days.
149 *Leviticus 11:2 -* **Searching for prescribed signs in beasts, for eating.**
Speak unto the children of Israel, saying, These are the beasts which ye shall eat among all the beasts that are on the earth.
150 *Deuteronomy 14:11 -* **Searching for the prescribed signs in birds, for eating.**
Of all clean birds ye shall eat.
151 *Leviticus 11:21 -* **Searching for prescribed signs in locusts, for eating.**
Yet these may ye eat of every flying creeping thing that goeth upon all four, which have legs above their feet, to leap withal upon the earth;
152 *Leviticus 11:9 -* **Searching for the prescribed signs in fish, for eating.**
These shall ye eat of all that are in the waters: whatsoever hath fins and scales in the waters, in the seas, and in the rivers, them shall ye eat.

FESTIVALS

153 *Exodus 12:2 -* **Sanhedrin to sanctify New Moon, and reckon years and seasons.**
This month shall be unto you the beginning of months: it shall be the first month of the year to you.
154 *Exodus 23:12 -* **On resting on the Shabbat.**
Six days thou shalt do thy work, and on the seventh day thou shalt

rest: that thine ox and thine ass may rest, and the son of thy handmaid, and the stranger, may be refreshed.

155 *Exodus 20:8 - **On declaring Shabbat holy at its onset and termination.***

Remember the sabbath day, to keep it holy.

156 *Exodus 12:15 - **On removal of chametz (leaven), on (Nisan 14th) Pesach (Passover).***

Seven days shall ye eat unleavened bread; even the first day ye shall put away leaven out of your houses: for whosoever eateth leavened bread from the first day until the seventh day, that soul shall be cut off from Israel.

157 *Exodus 13:8 - **Tell of Exodus from Egypt 1st night Pesach (Passover), (Nisan 15th).***

And thou shalt shew thy son in that day, saying, This is done because of that which the LORD did unto me when I came forth out of Egypt.

158 *Exodus 12:18 - **On eating Matzah the first night of Pesach (Passover), (Nisan 15th).***

In the first month, on the fourteenth day of the month at even, ye shall eat unleavened bread, until the one and twentieth day of the month at even.

159 *Exodus 12:16 - **On resting on the first day of Pesach (Passover).***

And in the first day there shall be an holy convocation, and in the seventh day there shall be an holy convocation to you; no manner of work shall be done in them, save that which every man must eat, that only may be done of you.

160 *Exodus 12:16 - **On resting on the seventh day of Pesach (Passover).***

And in the first day there shall be an holy convocation, and in the seventh day there shall be an holy convocation to you; no manner of work shall be done in them, save that which every man must eat, that only may be done of you.

161 Leviticus 23:15 - **Count the Omer (Counting) 49 days from day of first sheaf, Nisan 16.**

And ye shall count unto you from the morrow after the sabbath, from the day that ye brought the sheaf of the wave offering; seven sabbaths shall be complete:

162 Leviticus 23:21 - **On resting on Shavuot (Pentecost).**

And ye shall proclaim on the selfsame day, that it may be an holy convocation unto you: ye shall do no servile work therein: it shall be a statute for ever in all your dwellings throughout your generations.

163 Leviticus 23:24 - **On resting on Rosh HaShannah (Head of Year).**

Speak unto the children of Israel, saying, In the seventh month, in the first day of the month, shall ye have a sabbath, a memorial of blowing of trumpets, an holy convocation.

164 Leviticus 16:29 - **On fasting on Yom Kippur (Day of Atonement).**

And this shall be a statute for ever unto you: that in the seventh month, on the tenth day of the month, ye shall afflict your souls, and do no work at all, whether it be one of your own country, or a stranger that sojourneth among you:

165 Leviticus 16:29 - **On resting on Yom Kippur.**

And this shall be a statute for ever unto you: that in the seventh month, on the tenth day of the month, ye shall afflict your souls, and do no work at all, whether it be one of your own country, or a stranger that sojourneth among you:

166 Leviticus 23:35 - **On resting on the first day of Sukkot.**

On the first day shall be an holy convocation: ye shall do no servile work therein.

167 Leviticus 23:36 - **On resting on (the 8th day) Shemini Atzeret.**

Seven days ye shall offer an offering made by fire unto the LORD: on the eighth day shall be an holy convocation unto you; and ye shall offer an offering made by fire unto the LORD: it is a solemn assembly; and ye shall do no servile work therein.

168 Leviticus 23:42 - **On dwelling in a Sukkah (Booths) for seven days.**

Ye shall dwell in booths seven days; all that are Israelites born shall dwell in booths:

169 Leviticus 23:40 - **On taking a Lulav (the four species) on Sukkot.**

And ye shall take you on the first day the boughs of goodly trees, branches of palm trees, and the boughs of thick trees, and willows of the brook; and ye shall rejoice before the LORD your God seven days.

170 Numbers 29:1 - **On hearing the sound of the Shofar on Rosh HaShannah (Head of Year).**

And in the seventh month, on the first day of the month, ye shall have an holy convocation; ye shall do no servile work: it is a day of blowing the trumpets unto you.

COMMUNITY

171 Exodus 30:12 - **On every male giving half a shekel annually to Temple.**

When thou takest the sum of the children of Israel after their number, then shall they give every man a ransom for his soul unto the LORD, when thou numberest them; that there be no plague among them, when thou numberest them.

172 Deuteronomy 18:15 - **On heeding the Prophets.**

The LORD thy God will raise up unto thee a Prophet from the midst of thee, of thy brethren, like unto me; unto him ye shall hearken;

173 *Deuteronomy 17:15 -* **On appointing a king.**

Thou shalt in any wise set him king over thee, whom the LORD thy God shall choose: one from among thy brethren shalt thou set king over thee: thou mayest not set a stranger over thee, which is not thy brother.

174 *Deuteronomy 17:11 -* **On obeying the Great Court (Sanhedrin).**

According to the sentence of the law which they shall teach thee, and according to the judgment which they shall tell thee, thou shalt do: thou shalt not decline from the sentence which they shall shew thee, to the right hand, nor to the left.

175 *Exodus 23:2 -* **On in case of division, abiding by a majority decision.**

Thou shalt not follow a multitude to do evil; neither shalt thou speak in a cause to decline after many to wrest judgment:

176 *Deuteronomy 16:18 -* **Appointing Judges and Officers of the Court in every town.**

Judges and officers shalt thou make thee in all thy gates, which the LORD thy God giveth thee, throughout thy tribes: and they shall judge the people with just judgment.

177 *Leviticus 19:15 -* **Treating litigants equally / impartially before the law.**

Ye shall do no unrighteousness in judgment: thou shalt not respect the person of the poor, nor honour the person of the mighty: but in righteousness shalt thou judge thy neighbour.

178 *Leviticus 5:1 -* **Anyone aware of evidence must come to court to testify.**

And if a soul sin, and hear the voice of swearing, and is a witness, whether he hath seen or known of it; if he do not utter it, then he shall bear his iniquity.

179 *Deuteronomy 13:14 -* **The testimony of witnesses shall be examined thoroughly.**

Then shalt thou enquire, and make search, and ask diligently; and, behold, if it be truth, and the thing certain, that such abomination is wrought among you;

180 *Deuteronomy 19:19 -* **False witnesses punished, as they intended upon accused.**

Then shall ye do unto him, as he had thought to have done unto his brother: so shalt thou put the evil away from among you.

181 *Deuteronomy 21:4 -* **On Eglah Arufah, on the heifer when murderer unknown.**

And the elders of that city shall bring down the heifer unto a rough valley, which is neither eared nor sown, and shall strike off the heifer's neck there in the valley:

182 *Deuteronomy 19:3 -* **On establishing Six Cities of Refuge.**

Thou shalt prepare thee a way, and divide the coasts of thy land, which the LORD thy God giveth thee to inherit, into three parts, that every slayer may flee thither.

183 *Numbers 35:2 -* **Give cities to Levites - who've no ancestral land share.**

Command the children of Israel, that they give unto the Levites of the inheritance of their possession cities to dwell in; and ye shall give also unto the Levites suburbs for the cities round about them.

184 *Deuteronomy 22:8 -* **Build fence on roof, remove potential hazards from home.**

When thou buildest a new house, then thou shalt make a battlement for thy roof, that thou bring not blood upon thine house, if any man fall from thence.

IDOLATRY

185 *Deuteronomy 12:2 -* **On destroying all idolatry and its appurtenances.**
Ye shall utterly destroy all the places, wherein the nations which ye shall possess served their gods, upon the high mountains, and upon the hills, and under every green tree:

186 *Deuteronomy 13:16 -* **The law about a city that has become apostate / perverted.**
And thou shalt gather all the spoil of it into the midst of the street thereof, and shalt burn with fire the city, and all the spoil thereof every whit, for the LORD thy God: and it shall be an heap for ever; it shall not be built again.

187 *Deuteronomy 20:17 -* **On the law about destroying the seven Canaanite nations.**
But thou shalt utterly destroy them; namely, the Hittites, and the Amorites, the Canaanites, and the Perizzites, the Hivites, and the Jebusites; as the LORD thy God hath commanded thee:

188 *Deuteronomy 25:19 -* **On the extinction of the seed of Amalek.**
Therefore it shall be, when the LORD thy God hath given thee rest from all thine enemies round about, in the land which the LORD thy God giveth thee for an inheritance to possess it, that thou shalt blot out the remembrance of Amalek from under heaven; thou shalt not forget it.

189 *Deuteronomy 25:17 -* **On remembering the evil deeds of Amalek to Israel.**
Remember what Amalek did unto thee by the way, when ye were come forth out of Egypt;

WAR

190 *Deuteronomy 20:11* - **Regulations for wars other than ones commanded in Torah.**

And it shall be, if it make thee answer of peace, and open unto thee, then it shall be, that all the people that is found therein shall be tributaries unto thee, and they shall serve thee.

191 *Deuteronomy 20:2* - **Cohen for special duties in war.**

And it shall be, when ye are come nigh unto the battle, that the priest shall approach and speak unto the people,

192 *Deuteronomy 23:14* - **Prepare place beyond the camp, so to keep sanitary and...**

For the LORD thy God walketh in the midst of thy camp, to deliver thee, and to give up thine enemies before thee; therefore shall thy camp be holy: that he see no unclean thing in thee, and turn away from thee.

193 *Deuteronomy 23:13* - **...so include a digging tool among war implements.**

And thou shalt have a paddle upon thy weapon; and it shall be, when thou wilt ease thyself abroad, thou shalt dig therewith, and shalt turn back and cover that which cometh from thee:

SOCIAL

194 *Leviticus 6:4* - **On a robber to restore the stolen article to its owner.**

Then it shall be, because he hath sinned, and is guilty, that he shall restore that which he took violently away, or the thing which he hath deceitfully gotten, or that which was delivered him to keep, or the lost thing which he found,

195 *Deuteronomy 15:8* - **On to give charity to the poor.**

But thou shalt open thine hand wide unto him, and shalt surely lend him sufficient for his need, in that which he wanteth.

196 Deuteronomy 15:14 - **On giving gifts to a Hebrew bondman upon his freedom.**

Thou shalt furnish him liberally out of thy flock, and out of thy floor, and out of thy winepress: of that wherewith the LORD thy God hath blessed thee thou shalt give unto him.

197 Exodus 22:25 - **On lending money to the poor without interest.**

If thou lend money to any of my people that is poor by thee, thou shalt not be to him as an usurer, neither shalt thou lay upon him usury.

198 Deuteronomy 23:20 - **On lending money to the foreigner with interest.**

Unto a stranger thou mayest lend upon usury; but unto thy brother thou shalt not lend upon usury: that the LORD thy God may bless thee in all that thou settest thine hand to in the land whither thou goest to possess it.

199 Deuteronomy 24:13 - **On restoring a pledge to its owner if he needs it.**

In any case thou shalt deliver him the pledge again when the sun goeth down, that he may sleep in his own raiment, and bless thee: and it shall be righteousness unto thee before the LORD thy God.

200 Deuteronomy 24:15 - **On paying the worker his wages on time.**

At his day thou shalt give him his hire, neither shall the sun go down upon it; for he is poor, and setteth his heart upon it: lest he cry against thee unto the LORD, and it be sin unto thee.

201 Deuteronomy 23:24 - **Employee is allowed to eat the produce he's working in.**

When thou comest into thy neighbour's vineyard, then thou

mayest eat grapes thy fill at thine own pleasure; but thou shalt not put any in thy vessel.

202 *Exodus 23:5 -* **On helping unload when necessary a tired animal.**

If thou see the ass of him that hateth thee lying under his burden, and wouldest forbear to help him, thou shalt surely help with him.

203 *Deuteronomy 22:4 -* **On assisting a man loading his beast with its burden.**

Thou shalt not see thy brother's ass or his ox fall down by the way, and hide thyself from them: thou shalt surely help him to lift them up again.

204 *Deuteronomy 22:1 -* **On that lost property must be returned to its owner.**

Thou shalt not see thy brother's ox or his sheep go astray, and hide thyself from them: thou shalt in any case bring them again unto thy brother.

205 *Leviticus 19:17 -* **On being required to reprove the sinner.**

Thou shalt not hate thy brother in thine heart: thou shalt in any wise rebuke thy neighbour, and not suffer sin upon him.

206 *Leviticus 19:18 -* **On love your neighbor as yourself.**

Thou shalt not avenge, nor bear any grudge against the children of thy people, but thou shalt love thy neighbour as thyself: I am the LORD.

207 *Deuteronomy 10:19 -* **On being commanded to love the convert / proselyte.**

Love ye therefore the stranger: for ye were strangers in the land of Egypt.

208 *Leviticus 19:36 -* **On the law of accurate weights and measures.**

Just balances, just weights, a just ephah, and a just hin, shall ye

*have: I am the LORD your God, which brought you out of the
land of Egypt.*

FAMILY

209 *Leviticus 19:32 -* ***On honoring the old (and wise).***
*Thou shalt rise up before the hoary head, and honour the face of
the old man, and fear thy God: I am the LORD.*
210 *Exodus 20:12 -* ***On honoring parents.***
*Honour thy father and thy mother: that thy days may be long
upon the land which the LORD thy God giveth thee.*
211 *Leviticus19:3 -* ***On fearing parents.***
*Ye shall fear every man his mother, and his father, and keep my
sabbaths: I am the LORD your God.*
212 *Genesis1:28 -* ***On to be fruitful and multiply.***
*And God blessed them, and God said unto them, Be fruitful, and
multiply, and replenish the earth, and subdue it: and have
dominion over the fish of the sea, and over the fowl of the air, and
over every living thing that moveth upon the earth.*
213 *Deuteronomy 24:1 -* ***On the law of marriage.***
*When a man hath taken a wife, and married her, and it come to
pass that she find no favour in his eyes, because he hath found
some uncleanness in her: then let him write her a bill of
divorcement, and give it in her hand, and send her out of his
house.*
214 *Deuteronomy 24:5 -* ***On bridegroom devotes himself to his
wife for one year.***
*When a man hath taken a new wife, he shall not go out to war,
neither shall he be charged with any business: but he shall be
free at home one year, and shall cheer up his wife which he hath
taken.*

215 *Genesis 17:10 -* **On circumcising one's son.**

This is my covenant, which ye shall keep, between me and you and thy seed after thee; Every man child among you shall be circumcised.

216 *Deuteronomy 25:5 -* **If a man dies childless his brother marry widow, or...**

If brethren dwell together, and one of them die, and have no child, the wife of the dead shall not marry without unto a stranger: her husband's brother shall go in unto her, and take her to him to wife, and perform the duty of an husband's brother unto her.

217 *Deuteronomy 25:9 -* **...release her / the-widow Chalitzah.**

Then shall his brother's wife come unto him in the presence of the elders, and loose his shoe from off his foot, and spit in his face, and shall answer and say, So shall it be done unto that man that will not build up his brother's house.

218 *Deuteronomy 22:29 -* **A violator must marry the virgin / maiden he has violated.**

Then the man that lay with her shall give unto the damsel's father fifty shekels of silver, and she shall be his wife; because he hath humbled her, he may not put her away all his days.

219 *Deuteronomy 22:18 -* **The defamer of his bride is flogged and may never divorce.**

And the elders of that city shall take that man and chastise him;

220 *Exodus 22:16 -* **On the seducer must be punished according to the law.**

And if a man entice a maid that is not betrothed, and lie with her, he shall surely endow her to be his wife.

221 *Deuteronomy 21:11 -* **Captive women treated according to special regulations.**

And seest among the captives a beautiful woman, and hast a desire unto her, that thou wouldest have her to thy wife;

222 *Deuteronomy 24:1 -* **The law of divorce, only be means of written document.**

When a man hath taken a wife, and married her, and it come to pass that she find no favour in his eyes, because he hath found some uncleanness in her: then let him write her a bill of divorcement, and give it in her hand, and send her out of his house.

223 *Numbers 5:15 -* **Suspected adulteress has to submit to the required test.**

Then shall the man bring his wife unto the priest, and he shall bring her offering for her, the tenth part of an ephah of barley meal; he shall pour no oil upon it, nor put frankincense thereon; for it is an offering of jealousy, an offering of memorial, bringing iniquity to remembrance.

JUDICIAL

224 *Deuteronomy 25:2 -* **On whipping transgressors of certain commandments.**

And it shall be, if the wicked man be worthy to be beaten, that the judge shall cause him to lie down, and to be beaten before his face, according to his fault, by a certain number.

225 *Numbers 35:25 -* **On exile to city of refuge for unintentional homicide.**

And the congregation shall deliver the slayer out of the hand of the revenger of blood, and the congregation shall restore him to the city of his refuge, whither he was fled: and he shall abide in it unto the death of the high priest, which was anointed with the holy oil.

226 *Exodus 21:20 -* **On punishment of transgressors of certain commandments.**

And if a man smite his servant, or his maid, with a rod, and he die under his hand; he shall be surely punished.

227 *Exodus 21:16 -* **On strangling transgressors of certain commandments.**

And he that stealeth a man, and selleth him, or if he be found in his hand, he shall surely be put to death.

228 *Leviticus 20:14 -* **On burning transgressors of certain commandments.**

And if a man take a wife and her mother, it is wickedness: they shall be burnt with fire, both he and they; that there be no wickedness among you.

229 *Deuteronomy 22:24 -* **On stoning transgressors of certain commandments.**

Then ye shall bring them both out unto the gate of that city, and ye shall stone them with stones that they die; the damsel, because she cried not, being in the city; and the man, because he hath humbled his neighbour's wife: so thou shalt put away evil from among you.

230 *Deuteronomy 21:22 -* **Hang after execution, violators of certain commandments.**

And if a man have committed a sin worthy of death, and he be to be put to death, and thou hang him on a tree:

231 *Deuteronomy 21:23 -* **On burial on the same day of execution.**

His body shall not remain all night upon the tree, but thou shalt in any wise bury him that day; (for he that is hanged is accursed of God;) that thy land be not defiled, which the LORD thy God giveth thee for an inheritance.

SLAVES

232 Exodus 21:2 - **On the special laws for treating the Hebrew bondman.**
If thou buy an Hebrew servant, six years he shall serve: and in the seventh he shall go out free for nothing.

233 Exodus 21:8, 9 - **Hebrew bondmaid married to her master or his son, or...**
If she please not her master, who hath betrothed her to himself, then shall he let her be redeemed: to sell her unto a strange nation he shall have no power, seeing he hath dealt deceitfully with her. And if he have betrothed her unto his son, he shall deal with her after the manner of daughters.

234 Exodus 21:9 - **...allow the redemption to the Hebrew bondmaid.**
And if he have betrothed her unto his son, he shall deal with her after the manner of daughters.

235 Leviticus 25:46 - **On the laws for treating an alien bondman.**
And ye shall take them as an inheritance for your children after you, to inherit them for a possession; they shall be your bondmen for ever: but over your brethren the children of Israel, ye shall not rule one over another with rigour.

TORTS

236 Exodus 21:19 - **On the penalty for a person inflicting injury.**
If he rise again, and walk abroad upon his staff, then shall he that smote him be quit: only he shall pay for the loss of his time, and shall cause him to be thoroughly healed.

237 *Exodus 21:28 -* **On the law of injuries caused by an animal.**
If an ox gore a man or a woman, that they die: then the ox shall be surely stoned, and his flesh shall not be eaten; but the owner of the ox shall be quit.

238 *Exodus 21:33 -* **On the law of injuries caused by an pit.**
And if a man shall open a pit, or if a man shall dig a pit, and not cover it, and an ox or an ass fall therein;

239 *Exodus 22:1 -* **On the law of punishment of thieves.**
If a man shall steal an ox, or a sheep, and kill it, or sell it; he shall restore five oxen for an ox, and four sheep for a sheep.

240 *Exodus 22:5 -* **On the law of a judgement for damage caused by a beast.**
If a man shall cause a field or vineyard to be eaten, and shall put in his beast, and shall feed in another man's field; of the best of his own field, and of the best of his own vineyard, shall he make restitution.

241 *Exodus 22:6 -* **On the law of a judgement for damage caused by a fire.**
If fire break out, and catch in thorns, so that the stacks of corn, or the standing corn, or the field, be consumed therewith; he that kindled the fire shall surely make restitution.

242 *Exodus 22:7 -* **On the law of an unpaid guardian.**
If a man shall deliver unto his neighbour money or stuff to keep, and it be stolen out of the man's house; if the thief be found, let him pay double.

243 *Exodus 22:11 -* **On the law of a paid guardian.**
Then shall an oath of the LORD be between them both, that he hath not put his hand unto his neighbour's goods; and the owner of it shall accept thereof, and he shall not make it good.

244 *Exodus 22:14 -* **On the law of a borrower.**
And if a man borrow ought of his neighbour, and it be hurt, or

die, the owner thereof being not with it, he shall surely make it good.

245 Leviticus 25:14 - **On the law of buying and selling.**
And if thou sell ought unto thy neighbour, or buyest ought of thy neighbour's hand, ye shall not oppress one another:

246 Exodus 22:9 - **On the law of litigants.**
For all manner of trespass, whether it be for ox, for ass, for sheep, for raiment, or for any manner of lost thing, which another challengeth to be his, the cause of both parties shall come before the judges; and whom the judges shall condemn, he shall pay double unto his neighbour.

247 Deuteronomy 25:1 - **Save life of one pursued.**
If there be a controversy between men, and they come unto judgment, that the judges may judge them; then they shall justify the righteous, and condemn the wicked.

248 Numbers 27:8 - **On the law of inheritance.**
And thou shalt speak unto the children of Israel, saying, If a man die, and have no son, then ye shall cause his inheritance to pass unto his daughter.

The 365 Negative Mizvot/ Commandments: "The Don'ts"

IDOLATRY AND RELATED PRACTICES

1 Exodus 20:3 - **No other gods before me.**
Thou shalt have no other gods before me.

2 Exodus 20:4 - **Not to make graven images.**
Thou shalt not make unto thee any graven image, or any likeness of any thing that is in heaven above, or that is in the earth beneath, or that is in the water under the earth:

3 Leviticus 19:4 - **Not to make an idol (even for others) to**

worship.

Turn ye not unto idols, nor make to yourselves molten gods: I am the LORD your God.

*4 Exodus 20:4 - **Not to make figures of human beings.***

Thou shalt not make unto thee any graven image, or any likeness of any thing that is in heaven above, or that is in the earth beneath, or that is in the water under the earth:

*5 Exodus 20:5 - **Not to bow down to an idol.***

Thou shalt not bow down thyself to them, nor serve them: for I the LORD thy God am a jealous God, visiting the iniquity of the fathers upon the children unto the third and fourth generation of them that hate me;

*6 Exodus 20:5 - **Not to serve idols.***

Thou shalt not bow down thyself to them, nor serve them: for I the LORD thy God am a jealous God, visiting the iniquity of the fathers upon the children unto the third and fourth generation of them that hate me;

*7 Leviticus 18:21 - **Not to hand over any children to Molech***

And thou shalt not let any of thy seed pass through the fire to Molech, neither shalt thou profane the name of thy God: I am the LORD.

*8 Leviticus 19:31 - **Not to seek after wizards.***

Regard not them that have familiar spirits, neither seek after wizards, to be defiled by them: I am the LORD your God.

*9 Leviticus 19:31 - **Not to regard them that have familiar spirits.***

Regard not them that have familiar spirits, neither seek after wizards, to be defiled by them: I am the LORD your God.

*10 Leviticus 19:4 - **Not to study idolatrous practices.***

Turn ye not unto idols, nor make to yourselves molten gods: I am the LORD your God.

*11 Deuteronomy 16:22 - **Not to erect an image which people*** *assemble to honor.*

Neither shalt thou set thee up any image; which the LORD thy God hateth.

12 *Leviticus 26:1 -* **No figured stones to bow down to.**

Ye shall make you no idols nor graven image, neither rear you up a standing image, neither shall ye set up any image of stone in your land, to bow down unto it: for I am the LORD your God.

13 *Deuteronomy 16:21 -* **Not to plant trees near the altar.**

Thou shalt not plant thee a grove of any trees near unto the altar of the LORD thy God, which thou shalt make thee.

14 *Exodus 23:13 -* **Make no mention of other gods.**

And in all things that I have said unto you be circumspect: and make no mention of the name of other gods, neither let it be heard out of thy mouth.

15 *Exodus 23:13 -* **Not to divert anyone to idolatry.**

And in all things that I have said unto you be circumspect: and make no mention of the name of other gods, neither let it be heard out of thy mouth.

16 *Deuteronomy 13:12, 13 -* **Not to try to persuade a Jew to worship idols.**

If thou shalt hear say in one of thy cities, which the LORD thy God hath given thee to dwell there, saying, Certain men, the children of Belial, are gone out from among you, and have withdrawn the inhabitants of their city, saying, Let us go and serve other gods, which ye have not known;

17 *Deuteronomy 13:8 -* **Not to love someone who seeks to mislead you to idols.**

Thou shalt not consent unto him, nor hearken unto him; neither shall thine eye pity him, neither shalt thou spare, neither shalt thou conceal him:

18 *Deuteronomy 13:9 -* **Not to relax one's aversion to the**

misleader to idols.

But thou shalt surely kill him; thine hand shall be first upon him to put him to death, and afterwards the hand of all the people.

19 *Deuteronomy 13:9* - **Not to save the life of a misleader to idols.**

But thou shalt surely kill him; thine hand shall be first upon him to put him to death, and afterwards the hand of all the people.

20 *Deuteronomy 13:9* - **Not to plead for (defend) the misleader to idols.**

But thou shalt surely kill him; thine hand shall be first upon him to put him to death, and afterwards the hand of all the people.

21 *Deuteronomy 13:9* - **Not to oppress evidence unfavorable to the misleader.**

But thou shalt surely kill him; thine hand shall be first upon him to put him to death, and afterwards the hand of all the people.

22 *Deuteronomy 7:25* - **No benefit from ornaments which have adorned an idol.**

The graven images of their gods shall ye burn with fire: thou shalt not desire the silver or gold that is on them, nor take it unto thee, lest thou be snared therein: for it is an abomination to the LORD thy God.

23 *Deuteronomy 13:16* - **Rebuild not a city destroyed as punishment for idolatry.**

And thou shalt gather all the spoil of it into the midst of the street thereof, and shalt burn with fire the city, and all the spoil thereof every whit, for the LORD thy God: and it shall be an heap for ever; it shall not be built again.

24 *Deuteronomy 13:17* - **Not deriving benefit from property of an apostate city.**

And there shall cleave nought of the cursed thing to thine hand: that the LORD may turn from the fierceness of his anger, and shew thee mercy, and have compassion upon thee, and multiply thee, as he hath sworn unto thy fathers;

25 Deuteronomy 7:26 - **Do not use anything connected with idols or idolatry.**

Neither shalt thou bring an abomination into thine house, lest thou be a cursed thing like it: but thou shalt utterly detest it, and thou shalt utterly abhor it; for it is a cursed thing.

26 Deuteronomy 18:20 - **Not prophesying in the name of idols.**

But the prophet, which shall presume to speak a word in my name, which I have not commanded him to speak, or that shall speak in the name of other gods, even that prophet shall die.

27 Deuteronomy 18:20 - **Not prophesying falsely in the Name of God.**

But the prophet, which shall presume to speak a word in my name, which I have not commanded him to speak, or that shall speak in the name of other gods, even that prophet shall die.

28 Deuteronomy 13:3 - **Listen not to one who prophesies in the name of idols.**

Thou shalt not hearken unto the words of that prophet, or that dreamer of dreams: for the LORD your God proveth you, to know whether ye love the LORD your God with all your heart and with all your soul.

29 Deuteronomy 18:20 - **Not fearing or refraining from killing a false prophet.**

But the prophet, which shall presume to speak a word in my name, which I have not commanded him to speak, or that shall speak in the name of other gods, even that prophet shall die.

30 Leviticus 20:23 - **Imitate not the ways nor practice customs of idolaters.**

And ye shall not walk in the manners of the nation, which I cast out before you: for they committed all these things, and therefore

I abhorred them.

31 *Leviticus 19:26 -* **Not practicing divination (Deuteronomy 18:10).**

Ye shall not eat any thing with the blood: neither shall ye use enchantment, nor observe times.

32 *Deuteronomy 18:10 -* **Not practicing soothsaying.**

There shall not be found among you any one that maketh his son or his daughter to pass through the fire, or that useth divination, or an observer of times, or an enchanter, or a witch,

33 *Deuteronomy 18:10 -* **Not practicing enchanting.**

There shall not be found among you any one that maketh his son or his daughter to pass through the fire, or that useth divination, or an observer of times, or an enchanter, or a witch,

34 *Deuteronomy 18:10 -* **Not practicing sorcery.**

There shall not be found among you any one that maketh his son or his daughter to pass through the fire, or that useth divination, or an observer of times, or an enchanter, or a witch,

35 *Deuteronomy 18:11 -* **Not practicing the art of the charmer.**

Or a charmer, or a consulter with familiar spirits, or a wizard, or a necromancer.

36 *Deuteronomy 18:10 -* **Not consulting a necromancer.**

There shall not be found among you any one that maketh his son or his daughter to pass through the fire, or that useth divination, or an observer of times, or an enchanter, or a witch,

37 *Deuteronomy 18:11 -* **Not consulting a sorcerer.**

Or a charmer, or a consulter with familiar spirits, or a wizard, or a necromancer.

38 *Deuteronomy 18:11 -* **Not to seek information from the dead, necromancy.**

Or a charmer, or a consulter with familiar spirits, or a wizard, or a necromancer.

39 Deuteronomy 22:5 - **Women not to wear men's clothes or adornments.**
The woman shall not wear that which pertaineth unto a man, neither shall a man put on a woman's garment: for all that do so are abomination unto the LORD thy God.

40 Deuteronomy 22:5 - **Men not wearing women's clothes or adornments.**
The woman shall not wear that which pertaineth unto a man, neither shall a man put on a woman's garment: for all that do so are abomination unto the LORD thy God.

41 Leviticus 19:28 - **Not tattoo yourself, as is the manner of the idolaters.**
Ye shall not make any cuttings in your flesh for the dead, nor print any marks upon you: I am the LORD.

42 Deuteronomy 22:11 - **Not wearing a mixture of wool and linen.**
Thou shalt not wear a garment of divers sorts, as of woollen and linen together.

43 Leviticus 19:27 - **Not shaving the temples or sides of your head.**
Ye shall not round the corners of your heads, neither shalt thou mar the corners of thy beard.

44 Leviticus 19:27 - **Not shaving the corners of your beard.**
Ye shall not round the corners of your heads, neither shalt thou mar the corners of thy beard.

45 Leviticus 19:28 - **Not making cuttings in your flesh over your dead.**
Ye shall not make any cuttings in your flesh for the dead, nor print any marks upon you: I am the LORD.

PROHIBITIONS RESULTING FROM HISTORICAL

EVENTS

*46 Deuteronomy 17:16 - **Not returning to Egypt to dwell there permanently.***
But he shall not multiply horses to himself, nor cause the people to return to Egypt, to the end that he should multiply horses: forasmuch as the LORD hath said unto you, Ye shall henceforth return no more that way.

*47 Numbers 15:39 - **Not to follow one's heart or eyes, straying to impurity.***
And it shall be unto you for a fringe, that ye may look upon it, and remember all the commandments of the LORD, and do them; and that ye seek not after your own heart and your own eyes, after which ye use to go a whoring:

*48 Exodus 23:32 - **Not to make a pact with the Seven Canaanite Nations.***
Thou shalt make no covenant with them, nor with their gods.

*49 Deuteronomy 20:16 - **Not to spare the life of the Seven Canaanite Nations.***
But of the cities of these people, which the LORD thy God doth give thee for an inheritance, thou shalt save alive nothing that breatheth:

*50 Deuteronomy 7:2 - **Not to show mercy to idolaters.***
And when the LORD thy God shall deliver them before thee; thou shalt smite them, and utterly destroy them; thou shalt make no covenant with them, nor shew mercy unto them:

*51 Exodus 23:33 - **No one serving false gods to settle in the Land of Israel.***
They shall not dwell in thy land, lest they make thee sin against me: for if thou serve their gods, it will surely be a snare unto thee.

*52 Deuteronomy 7:3 - **Not to intermarry with one serving false gods.***
Neither shalt thou make marriages with them; thy daughter thou shalt not give unto his son, nor his daughter shalt thou take unto thy son.

*53 Deuteronomy 23:3 - **Not to enter the congregation, an Ammonite or Moabite.***
An Ammonite or Moabite shall not enter into the congregation of the LORD; even to their tenth generation shall they not enter into the congregation of the LORD for ever:

*54 Deuteronomy 23:8 - **Exclude not marrying a descendant of Esau if a proselyte.***
The children that are begotten of them shall enter into the congregation of the LORD in their third generation.

*55 Deuteronomy 23:8 - **Not to exclude marrying an Egyptian who is a proselyte.***
The children that are begotten of them shall enter into the congregation of the LORD in their third generation.

*56 Deuteronomy 23:6 - **Not permitted to make peace with Ammon and Moab nations.***
Thou shalt not seek their peace nor their prosperity all thy days for ever.

*57 Deuteronomy 20:19 - **Not destroying fruit trees, even in time of war.***
When thou shalt besiege a city a long time, in making war against it to take it, thou shalt not destroy the trees thereof by forcing an axe against them: for thou mayest eat of them, and thou shalt not cut them down (for the tree of the field is man's life) to employ them in the siege:

*58 Deuteronomy 7:21 - **Not fearing the enemy in time of war.***
Thou shalt not be affrighted at them: for the LORD thy God is

among you, a mighty God and terrible.
59 *Deuteronomy 25:19 -* **Blot out the remembrance of Amalek.**
*Therefore it shall be, when the LORD thy God hath given thee
rest from all thine enemies round about, in the land which the
LORD thy God giveth thee for an inheritance to possess it, that
thou shalt blot out the remembrance of Amalek from under
heaven; thou shalt not forget it.*

BLASPHEMY

60 *Leviticus 24:16 -* **Not blaspheming the Holy Name of God.**
*And he that blasphemeth the name of the LORD, he shall surely
be put to death, and all the congregation shall certainly stone
him: as well the stranger, as he that is born in the land, when he
blasphemeth the name of the LORD, shall be put to death.*
61 *Leviticus 19:12 -* **Not violating an oath by the Holy Name.**
*And ye shall not swear by my name falsely, neither shalt thou
profane the name of thy God: I am the LORD.*
62 *Exodus 20:7 -* **Not taking the Holy Name in vain.**
*Thou shalt not take the name of the LORD thy God in vain; for
the LORD will not hold him guiltless that taketh his name in
vain.*
63 *Leviticus 22:32 -* **Not profaning the Holy Name of God.**
*Neither shall ye profane my holy name; but I will be hallowed
among the children of Israel: I am the LORD which hallow you,*
64 *Deuteronomy 6:16 -* **Not tempting God's promises and
warnings.**
*Ye shall not tempt the LORD your God, as ye tempted him in
Massah.*
65 *Deuteronomy 12:3,4 -* **Do not destroy houses of worship or
holy books of The LORD.**

And ye shall overthrow their altars, and break their pillars, and burn their groves with fire; and ye shall hew down the graven images of their gods, and destroy the names of them out of that place. Ye shall not do so unto the LORD your God.

66 Deuteronomy 21:23 - **Leave not body of executed criminal hanging overnight.**

His body shall not remain all night upon the tree, but thou shalt in any wise bury him that day; (for he that is hanged is accursed of God;) that thy land be not defiled, which the LORD thy God giveth thee for an inheritance.

TEMPLE

67 Numbers 18:5 - **Be not lax in guarding the Sanctuary.**

And ye shall keep the charge of the sanctuary, and the charge of the altar: that there be no wrath any more upon the children of Israel.

68 Leviticus 16:2 - **High Priest enter Sanctuary only at prescribed times.**

And the LORD said unto Moses, Speak unto Aaron thy brother, that he come not at all times into the holy place within the vail before the mercy seat, which is upon the ark; that he die not: for I will appear in the cloud upon the mercy seat.

69 Leviticus 21:23 - **Cohen (priest) with blemish come near to Altar.**

Only he shall not go in unto the vail, nor come nigh unto the altar, because he hath a blemish; that he profane not my sanctuaries: for I the LORD do sanctify them.

70 Leviticus 21:17 - **Cohen (priest) with a blemish not to minister in the Sanctuary.**

Speak unto Aaron, saying, Whosoever he be of thy seed in their generations that hath any blemish, let him not approach to offer the bread of his God.

71 *Leviticus 21:18 -* **Cohen (priest) with temporary blemish minister not in Sanctuary.**

For whatsoever man he be that hath a blemish, he shall not approach: a blind man, or a lame, or he that hath a flat nose, or any thing superfluous,

72 *Numbers 18:3 -* **Levites and Cohanim not to interchange in their functions.**

And they shall keep thy charge, and the charge of all the tabernacle: only they shall not come nigh the vessels of the sanctuary and the altar, that neither they, nor ye also, die.

73 *Leviticus 10:9 -* **Drunk persons may not enter Sanctuary or teach Torah.**

Do not drink wine nor strong drink, thou, nor thy sons with thee, when ye go into the tabernacle of the congregation, lest ye die: it shall be a statute for ever throughout your generations:

74 *Numbers 18:4 -* **A non-Cohen (priest) not to minister in Sanctuary.**

And they shall be joined unto thee, and keep the charge of the tabernacle of the congregation, for all the service of the tabernacle: and a stranger shall not come nigh unto you.

75 *Leviticus 22:2 -* **A unclean Cohen (priest) not to minister in Sanctuary.**

Speak unto Aaron and to his sons, that they separate themselves from the holy things of the children of Israel, and that they profane not my holy name in those things which they hallow unto me: I am the LORD.

76 *Leviticus 21:6 -* **A defiled Cohen (priest), not to minister in Sanctuary.**

They shall be holy unto their God, and not profane the name of their God: for the offerings of the LORD made by fire, and the bread of their God, they do offer: therefore they shall be holy.

77 *Numbers 5:2 - **A leper not to enter any part of Temple.***
Command the children of Israel, that they put out of the camp every leper, and every one that hath an issue, and whosoever is defiled by the dead:

78 *Deuteronomy 23:11 - **No unclean person may enter camp of Levites.***
But it shall be, when evening cometh on, he shall wash himself with water: and when the sun is down, he shall come into the camp again.

79 *Exodus 20:25 - **Build not an Altar of stones which were touched by iron.***
And if thou wilt make me an altar of stone, thou shalt not build it of hewn stone: for if thou lift up thy tool upon it, thou hast polluted it.

80 *Exodus 20:26 - **Not to have an ascent to the Altar by steps.***
Neither shalt thou go up by steps unto mine altar, that thy nakedness be not discovered thereon.

81 *Leviticus 6:13 - **Not to extinguish the Altar fire.***
The fire shall ever be burning upon the altar; it shall never go out.

82 *Exodus 30:9 - **Offer nothing, but specified incense, on Golden Altar.***
Ye shall offer no strange incense thereon, nor burnt sacrifice, nor meat offering; neither shall ye pour drink offering thereon.

83 *Exodus 30:32 - **Not to make any oil the same as the Oil of Anointment.***
Upon man's flesh shall it not be poured, neither shall ye make any other like it, after the composition of it: it is holy, and it shall be holy unto you.

84 *Exodus 30:32 - **Anoint none with special oil except Cohen Gadol (High Priest) and King.***

Upon man's flesh shall it not be poured, neither shall ye make any other like it, after the composition of it: it is holy, and it shall be holy unto you.

85 *Exodus 30:37 - **Not to make incense same as burnt on Altar in Sanctuary.***

And as for the perfume which thou shalt make, ye shall not make to yourselves according to the composition thereof: it shall be unto thee holy for the LORD.

86 *Exodus 25:15 - **Not to remove the staves from their rings in the Ark.***

The staves shall be in the rings of the ark: they shall not be taken from it.

87 *Exodus 28:28 - **Not to remove the Breastplate from the Ephod.***

And they shall bind the breastplate by the rings thereof unto the rings of the ephod with a lace of blue, that it may be above the curious girdle of the ephod, and that the breastplate be not loosed from the ephod.

88 *Exodus 28:32 - **Make not any incision in Cohen haGadol's (High Priest's) upper garment.***

And there shall be an hole in the top of it, in the midst thereof: it shall have a binding of woven work round about the hole of it, as it were the hole of an habergeon, that it be not rent.

SACRIFICES

89 *Deuteronomy 12:13 - **Offer not sacrifices outside Sanctuary (Temple) Court.***

Take heed to thyself that thou offer not thy burnt offerings in every place that thou seest:

90 *Leviticus 17:3-4 -* **Slaughter not consecrated animals outside Temple Court.**

What man soever there be of the house of Israel, that killeth an ox, or lamb, or goat, in the camp, or that killeth it out of the camp, And bringeth it not unto the door of the tabernacle of the congregation, to offer an offering unto the LORD before the tabernacle of the LORD; blood shall be imputed unto that man; he hath shed blood; and that man shall be cut off from among his people:

91 *Leviticus 22:20 -* **Dedicate not a blemished animal to be offered on Altar.**

But whatsoever hath a blemish, that shall ye not offer: for it shall not be acceptable for you.

92 *Leviticus 22:22 -* **Not to slaughter a blemished animal as a korban (sacrifice).** .

Blind, or broken, or maimed, or having a wen, or scurvy, or scabbed, ye shall not offer these unto the LORD, nor make an offering by fire of them upon the altar unto the LORD.

93 *Leviticus 22:24 -* **Not to dash the blood of a blemished beast on the Altar.**

Ye shall not offer unto the LORD that which is bruised, or crushed, or broken, or cut; neither shall ye make any offering thereof in your land.

94 *Leviticus 22:22 -* **Not to burn the inner parts of blemished beast on Altar.**

Blind, or broken, or maimed, or having a wen, or scurvy, or scabbed, ye shall not offer these unto the LORD, nor make an offering by fire of them upon the altar unto the LORD.

95 *Deuteronomy 17:1 -* **Not to sacrifice a beast with a temporary blemish.**

Thou shalt not sacrifice unto the LORD thy God any bullock, or sheep, wherein is blemish, or any evilfavouredness: for that is an abomination unto the LORD thy God.

96 *Leviticus 22:25 -* **Not to offer a blemished sacrifice of a gentile.**

Neither from a stranger's hand shall ye offer the bread of your God of any of these; because their corruption is in them, and blemishes be in them: they shall not be accepted for you.

97 *Leviticus 22:21 -* **Not to cause a consecrated offering to become blemished.**

And whosoever offereth a sacrifice of peace offerings unto the LORD to accomplish his vow, or a freewill offering in beeves or sheep, it shall be perfect to be accepted; there shall be no blemish therein.

98 *Leviticus 2:11 -* **Not to offer leaven or honey upon the Altar.**

No meat offering, which ye shall bring unto the LORD, shall be made with leaven: for ye shall burn no leaven, nor any honey, in any offering of the LORD made by fire.

99 *Leviticus 2:13 -* **Not to offer a sacrifice without salt.**

And every oblation of thy meat offering shalt thou season with salt; neither shalt thou suffer the salt of the covenant of thy God to be lacking from thy meat offering: with all thine offerings thou shalt offer salt.

100 *Deuteronomy 23:18 -* **Offer not on Altar: "hire of harlot" or "price of dog".**

Thou shalt not bring the hire of a whore, or the price of a dog, into the house of the LORD thy God for any vow: for even both these are abomination unto the LORD thy God.

101 *Leviticus 22:28 -* **Not to slaughter an animal and its young on the same day.**

And whether it be cow or ewe, ye shall not kill it and her young both in one day.

102 *Leviticus 5:11 -* **Not to put olive oil on the sin meal-offering.**

But if he be not able to bring two turtledoves, or two young pigeons, then he that sinned shall bring for his offering the tenth part of an ephah of fine flour for a sin offering; he shall put no oil upon it, neither shall he put any frankincense thereon: for it is a sin offering.

103 *Leviticus 5:11 -* **Not to put frankincense on the sin meal-offering.**

But if he be not able to bring two turtledoves, or two young pigeons, then he that sinned shall bring for his offering the tenth part of an ephah of fine flour for a sin offering; he shall put no oil upon it, neither shall he put any frankincense thereon: for it is a sin offering.

104 *Numbers 5:15 -* **Not to put olive oil on the jealousy offering.**

Then shall the man bring his wife unto the priest, and he shall bring her offering for her, the tenth part of an ephah of barley meal; he shall pour no oil upon it, nor put frankincense thereon; for it is an offering of jealousy, an offering of memorial, bringing iniquity to remembrance.

105 *Numbers 5:15 -* **Not to put frankincense on the jealousy offering.**

Then shall the man bring his wife unto the priest, and he shall bring her offering for her, the tenth part of an ephah of barley meal; he shall pour no oil upon it, nor put frankincense thereon; for it is an offering of jealousy, an offering of memorial, bringing iniquity to remembrance.

106 *Leviticus 27:10 -* **Not to substitute sacrifices.**

He shall not alter it, nor change it, a good for a bad, or a bad for a good: and if he shall at all change beast for beast, then it and the exchange thereof shall be holy.

107 *Leviticus 27:33 -* **Not to change sacrifices from one category to the other.**

He shall not search whether it be good or bad, neither shall he change it: and if he change it at all, then both it and the change thereof shall be holy; it shall not be redeemed.

108 *Numbers 18:17 -* **Redeem not the firstborn of permitted (clean) animals.**

But the firstling of a cow, or the firstling of a sheep, or the firstling of a goat, thou shalt not redeem; they are holy: thou shalt sprinkle their blood upon the altar, and shalt burn their fat for an offering made by fire, for a sweet savour unto the LORD.

109 *Leviticus 27:33 -* **Not to sell the tithe of the herd of cattle.**

He shall not search whether it be good or bad, neither shall he change it: and if he change it at all, then both it and the change thereof shall be holy; it shall not be redeemed.

110 *Leviticus 27:28 -* **Not to sell a devoted field.**

Notwithstanding no devoted thing, that a man shall devote unto the LORD of all that he hath, both of man and beast, and of the field of his possession, shall be sold or redeemed: every devoted thing is most holy unto the LORD.

111 *Leviticus 27:28 -* **Not to redeem a devoted (by the Cherem vow) field.**

Notwithstanding no devoted thing, that a man shall devote unto the LORD of all that he hath, both of man and beast, and of the field of his possession, shall be sold or redeemed: every devoted thing is most holy unto the LORD.

112 *Leviticus 5:8 -* **Not to split head of bird slaughtered for Sin-offering.**

And he shall bring them unto the priest, who shall offer that which is for the sin offering first, and wring off his head from his neck, but shall not divide it asunder:

113 *Deuteronomy 15:19 -* **Not to do any work with a dedicated beast.**

All the firstling males that come of thy herd and of thy flock thou shalt sanctify unto the LORD thy God: thou shalt do no work with the firstling of thy bullock, nor shear the firstling of thy sheep.

114 *Deuteronomy 15:19 -* **Not to shear a dedicated beast.**

All the firstling males that come of thy herd and of thy flock thou shalt sanctify unto the LORD thy God: thou shalt do no work with the firstling of thy bullock, nor shear the firstling of thy sheep.

115 *Exodus 34:25 -* **Slaughter not Pesach (Passover) lamb with chametz (leaven).**

Thou shalt not offer the blood of my sacrifice with leaven; neither shall the sacrifice of the feast of the passover be left unto the morning.

116 *Exodus 12:10 -* **Leave not sacrificial portions of Pesach (Passover) lamb overnight.**

And ye shall let nothing of it remain until the morning; and that which remaineth of it until the morning ye shall burn with fire.

117 *Exodus 12:10 -* **Allow not meat of Pesach (Passover) lamb to remain till morning.**

And ye shall let nothing of it remain until the morning; and that which remaineth of it until the morning ye shall burn with fire.

118 *Deuteronomy 16:4 -* **No meat of Nisan 14th Festive Offering remain till day 3.**

And there shall be no leavened bread seen with thee in all thy coast seven days; neither shall there any thing of the flesh, which thou sacrificedst the first day at even, remain all night until the morning.

119 *Numbers 9:12 -* **No meat of 2nd Pesach (Passover) lamb Offering remain till morning.**

They shall leave none of it unto the morning, nor break any bone of it: according to all the ordinances of the passover they shall keep it.

120 *Leviticus 22:30* - **No meat of Thanksgiving Offering to remain till morning.**

On the same day it shall be eaten up; ye shall leave none of it until the morrow: I am the LORD.

121 *Exodus 12:46* - **Not to break any bones of Pesach (Passover) lamb offering.**

In one house shall it be eaten; thou shalt not carry forth ought of the flesh abroad out of the house; neither shall ye break a bone thereof.

122 *Numbers 9:12* - **Not to break any bones of 2nd Pesach (Passover) lamb offering.**

They shall leave none of it unto the morning, nor break any bone of it: according to all the ordinances of the passover they shall keep it.

123 *Exodus 12:46* - **Not to remove Pesach (Passover) offering from where it is eaten.**

In one house shall it be eaten; thou shalt not carry forth ought of the flesh abroad out of the house; neither shall ye break a bone thereof.

124 *Leviticus 6:17* - **Not to bake the residue of a meal offering with leaven**

It shall not be baken with leaven. I have given it unto them for their portion of my offerings made by fire; it is most holy, as is the sin offering, and as the trespass offering.

125 *Exodus 12:9* - **Not to eat the Pesach (Passover) offering boiled or raw.**

Eat not of it raw, nor sodden at all with water, but roast with fire; his head with his legs, and with the purtenance thereof.

126 Exodus 12:45 - **Not to allow an alien resident to eat Pesach (Passover) offering.**
A foreigner and an hired servant shall not eat thereof.

127 Exodus 12:48 - **An uncircumcised person may not eat the Pesach (Passover) offering.**
And when a stranger shall sojourn with thee, and will keep the passover to the LORD, let all his males be circumcised, and then let him come near and keep it; and he shall be as one that is born in the land: for no uncircumcised person shall eat thereof.

128 Exodus 12:43 - **Not to allow an stranger to eat the Pesach (Passover) offering.**
And the LORD said unto Moses and Aaron, This is the ordinance of the passover: There shall no stranger eat thereof:

129 Leviticus 12:4 - **Tameh (ritually unclean) person may not eat holy things.**
And she shall then continue in the blood of her purifying three and thirty days; she shall touch no hallowed thing, nor come into the sanctuary, until the days of her purifying be fulfilled.

130 Leviticus 7:19 - **Eat not meat of consecrated things that have become unclean.**
And the flesh that toucheth any unclean thing shall not be eaten; it shall be burnt with fire: and as for the flesh, all that be clean shall eat thereof.

131 Leviticus 19:6,7 - **Not to eat sacrificial meat beyond the second day.**
It shall be eaten the same day ye offer it, and on the morrow: and if ought remain until the third day, it shall be burnt in the fire. And if it be eaten at all on the third day, it is abominable; it shall not be accepted.

132 Leviticus 7:18 - **Eat not sacrificial meat on third day.**
And if any of the flesh of the sacrifice of his peace offerings be

eaten at all on the third day, it shall not be accepted, neither shall it be imputed unto him that offereth it: it shall be an abomination, and the soul that eateth of it shall bear his iniquity.

133 *Leviticus 22:10 - **A stranger or non-Cohen may not eat of holy thing.***

There shall no stranger eat of the holy thing: a sojourner of the priest, or an hired servant, shall not eat of the holy thing.

134 *Leviticus 22:10 – **A Cohen 's (Priest's) sojourner or hired worker may not eat holy thing.***

There shall no stranger eat of the holy thing: a sojourner of the priest, or an hired servant, shall not eat of the holy thing.

135 *Leviticus 22:10 - **An uncircumcised person may not eat holy thing.***

There shall no stranger eat of the holy thing: a sojourner of the priest, or an hired servant, shall not eat of the holy thing.

136 *Leviticus 22:4 - **A Tameh (ritually unclean) Cohen may not eat terumah (holy things).***

What man soever of the seed of Aaron is a leper, or hath a running issue; he shall not eat of the holy things, until he be clean. And whoso toucheth any thing that is unclean by the dead, or a man whose seed goeth from him;

137 *Leviticus 22:12 - **A Bat-Cohen (priest's daughter) if married to non-Cohen not to eat holy food.***

If the priest's daughter also be married unto a stranger, she may not eat of an offering of the holy things.

138 *Leviticus 6:16 - **Not to eat the Meal-offering of a Cohen (Priest).***

And the remainder thereof shall Aaron and his sons eat: with unleavened bread shall it be eaten in the holy place; in the court of the tabernacle of the congregation they shall eat it.

139 *Leviticus 6:23 - **Eat not Sin-offering meat sacrificed within***

Sanctuary.

For every meat offering for the priest shall be wholly burnt: it shall not be eaten.

140 *Deuteronomy 14:3 -* **Not to eat consecrated animals that have become blemished.**

Thou shalt not eat any abominable thing.

141 *Deuteronomy 12:17 -* **Eat not unredeemed 2nd corn tithe outside Jerusalem.**

Thou mayest not eat within thy gates the tithe of thy corn, or of thy wine, or of thy oil, or the firstlings of thy herds or of thy flock, nor any of thy vows which thou vowest, nor thy freewill offerings, or heave offering of thine hand:

142 *Deuteronomy 12:17 -* **Consume not unredeemed 2nd wine tithe outside Jerusalem.**

Thou mayest not eat within thy gates the tithe of thy corn, or of thy wine, or of thy oil, or the firstlings of thy herds or of thy flock, nor any of thy vows which thou vowest, nor thy freewill offerings, or heave offering of thine hand:

143 *Deuteronomy 12:17 -* **Consume not unredeemed 2nd oil tithe outside Jerusalem.**

Thou mayest not eat within thy gates the tithe of thy corn, or of thy wine, or of thy oil, or the firstlings of thy herds or of thy flock, nor any of thy vows which thou vowest, nor thy freewill offerings, or heave offering of thine hand:

144 *Deuteronomy 12:17 -* **Eat not an unblemished firstling outside Jerusalem.**

Thou mayest not eat within thy gates the tithe of thy corn, or of thy wine, or of thy oil, or the firstlings of thy herds or of thy flock, nor any of thy vows which thou vowest, nor thy freewill offerings, or heave offering of thine hand:

145 *Deuteronomy 12:17 -* **Eat not sin or guilt offerings outside**

Sanctuary court.

Thou mayest not eat within thy gates the tithe of thy corn, or of thy wine, or of thy oil, or the firstlings of thy herds or of thy flock, nor any of thy vows which thou vowest, nor thy freewill offerings, or heave offering of thine hand:

146 *Deuteronomy 12:17 -* **Not to eat the meat of the burnt offering at all.**

Thou mayest not eat within thy gates the tithe of thy corn, or of thy wine, or of thy oil, or the firstlings of thy herds or of thy flock, nor any of thy vows which thou vowest, nor thy freewill offerings, or heave offering of thine hand:

147 *Deuteronomy 12:17 -* **Eat not lesser sacrifices before blood dashed on Altar.**

Thou mayest not eat within thy gates the tithe of thy corn, or of thy wine, or of thy oil, or the firstlings of thy herds or of thy flock, nor any of thy vows which thou vowest, nor thy freewill offerings, or heave offering of thine hand:

148 *Deuteronomy 12:17 -* **Azar / non- Cohen is not to eat the most holy offerings.**

Thou mayest not eat within thy gates the tithe of thy corn, or of thy wine, or of thy oil, or the firstlings of thy herds or of thy flock, nor any of thy vows which thou vowest, nor thy freewill offerings, or heave offering of thine hand:

149 *Exodus 29:33 -* **A Cohen (Priest) not to eat First Fruits outside Temple courts.**

And they shall eat those things wherewith the atonement was made, to consecrate and to sanctify them: but a stranger shall not eat thereof, because they are holy.

150 *Deuteronomy 26:14 -* **Not giving 2nd tithe while in state of impurity.**

I have not eaten thereof in my mourning, neither have I taken away ought thereof for any unclean use, nor given ought thereof for the dead: but I have hearkened to the voice of the LORD my God, and have done according to all that thou hast commanded me.

151 Deuteronomy 26:14 - **Not eating the 2nd tithe while in mourning.**

I have not eaten thereof in my mourning, neither have I taken away ought thereof for any unclean use, nor given ought thereof for the dead: but I have hearkened to the voice of the LORD my God, and have done according to all that thou hast commanded me.

152 Deuteronomy 26:14 - **Not giving the 2nd tithe for the dead.**

I have not eaten thereof in my mourning, neither have I taken away ought thereof for any unclean use, nor given ought thereof for the dead: but I have hearkened to the voice of the LORD my God, and have done according to all that thou hast commanded me.

153 Leviticus 22:15 - **Not eating untithed produce.**

And they shall not profane the holy things of the children of Israel, which they offer unto the LORD;

154 Exodus 22:29 - **Not changing the order of separating the various tithes.**

Thou shalt not delay to offer the first of thy ripe fruits, and of thy liquors: the firstborn of thy sons shalt thou give unto me.

155 Deuteronomy 23:21 - **Delay not payment of offerings, freewill or obligatory.**

When thou shalt vow a vow unto the LORD thy God, thou shalt not slack to pay it: for the LORD thy God will surely require it of thee; and it would be sin in thee.

156 Exodus 23:15 - **Go not to Temple on Passover, Pentecost and Tabernacles without offering.**

Thou shalt keep the feast of unleavened bread: (thou shalt eat unleavened bread seven days, as I commanded thee, in the time appointed of the month Abib; for in it thou camest out from Egypt: and none shall appear before me empty:)

157 *Numbers 30:2 -* **Not to break your word, even if without an oath.**

If a man vow a vow unto the LORD, or swear an oath to bind his soul with a bond; he shall not break his word, he shall do according to all that proceedeth out of his mouth.

PRIESTS

158 *Leviticus 21:7 -* **A Cohen (Priest) may not marry a harlot.**
They shall not take a wife that is a whore, or profane; neither shall they take a woman put away from her husband: for he is holy unto his God.

159 *Leviticus 21:7 -* **A Cohen (Priest) marry not a woman profaned from the Priesthood.**
They shall not take a wife that is a whore, or profane; neither shall they take a woman put away from her husband: for he is holy unto his God.

160 *Leviticus 21:7 -* **A Cohen (Priest) may not marry a divorcee.**
They shall not take a wife that is a whore, or profane; neither shall they take a woman put away from her husband: for he is holy unto his God.

161 *Leviticus 21:14 -* **Cohen haGadol (high priest) may not marry a widow.**
A widow, or a divorced woman, or profane, or an harlot, these shall he not take: but he shall take a virgin of his own people to wife.

162 *Leviticus 21:15 -* **Cohen haGadol (high priest) may not take**

a widow as a concubine.

Neither shall he profane his seed among his people: for I the LORD do sanctify him.

163 *Leviticus 10:6 -* **Cohen (Priest) may not enter the Sanctuary with uncovered head.**

And Moses said unto Aaron, and unto Eleazar and unto Ithamar, his sons, Uncover not your heads, neither rend your clothes; lest ye die, and lest wrath come upon all the people: but let your brethren, the whole house of Israel, bewail the burning which the LORD hath kindled.

164 *Leviticus 10:6 -* **Cohen (Priest) wearing rent garments may not enter Sanctuary.**

And Moses said unto Aaron, and unto Eleazar and unto Ithamar, his sons, Uncover not your heads, neither rend your clothes; lest ye die, and lest wrath come upon all the people: but let your brethren, the whole house of Israel, bewail the burning which the LORD hath kindled.

165 *Leviticus 10:7 –* **Cohanim (Priests) leave not Temple courtyard during the service.**

And ye shall not go out from the door of the tabernacle of the congregation, lest ye die: for the anointing oil of the LORD is upon you. And they did according to the word of Moses.

166 *Leviticus 21:1 -* **No Cohanim (Priests) must not be defiled for dead, except for his next of kin.**

And the LORD said unto Moses, Speak unto the priests the sons of Aaron, and say unto them, There shall none be defiled for the dead among his people:

167 *Leviticus 21:11 -* **Cohen haGadol (High Priest) may not be under one roof with dead body.**

Neither shall he go in to any dead body, nor defile himself for his father, or for his mother;

168 *Leviticus 21:11 -* **Cohen haGadol (High Priest) must not be defiled for any dead person.**
Neither shall he go in to any dead body, nor defile himself for his father, or for his mother;
169 *Deuteronomy 18:1 -* **Levites have not part in the division of Israel's land.**
The priests the Levites, and all the tribe of Levi, shall have no part nor inheritance with Israel: they shall eat the offerings of the LORD made by fire, and his inheritance.
170 *Deuteronomy 18:1 -* **Levites share not in the spoils of war.**
The priests the Levites, and all the tribe of Levi, shall have no part nor inheritance with Israel: they shall eat the offerings of the LORD made by fire, and his inheritance.
171 *Deuteronomy 14:1 -* **Not to tear out hair for the dead.**
Ye are the children of the LORD your God: ye shall not cut yourselves, nor make any baldness between your eyes for the dead.

DIETARY LAWS

172 *Deuteronomy 14:7 -* **Not to eat any unclean animal.**
Nevertheless these ye shall not eat of them that chew the cud, or of them that divide the cloven hoof; as the camel, and the hare, and the coney: for they chew the cud, but divide not the hoof; therefore they are unclean unto you.
173 *Leviticus 11:11 -* **Not to eat any unclean fish.**
They shall be even an abomination unto you; ye shall not eat of their flesh, but ye shall have their carcases in abomination.
174 *Leviticus 11:13 -* **Not to eat any unclean fowl.**
And these are they which ye shall have in abomination among the fowls; they shall not be eaten, they are an abomination: the eagle,

and the ossifrage, and the ospray,

175 *Deuteronomy 14:19* - **Not to eat any creeping winged insect.**

And every creeping thing that flieth is unclean unto you: they shall not be eaten.

176 *Leviticus 11:41* - **Not to eat anything which creeps on the earth.**

And every creeping thing that creepeth upon the earth shall be an abomination; it shall not be eaten.

177 *Leviticus 11:44* - **Not to eat creeping thing that is undefiled.**

For I am the LORD your God: ye shall therefore sanctify yourselves, and ye shall be holy; for I am holy: neither shall ye defile yourselves with any manner of creeping thing that creepeth upon the earth.

178 *Leviticus 11:42* - **Not to eat living creatures that goeth on belly.**

Whatsoever goeth upon the belly, and whatsoever goeth upon all four, or whatsoever hath more feet among all creeping things that creep upon the earth, them ye shall not eat; for they are an abomination.

179 *Leviticus 11:43* - **Not to eat any abominable creature.**

Ye shall not make yourselves abominable with any creeping thing that creepeth, neither shall ye make yourselves unclean with them, that ye should be defiled thereby.

180 *Deuteronomy 14:21* - **Not to eat any animal which died naturally, a nevelah.**

Ye shall not eat of any thing that dieth of itself: thou shalt give it unto the stranger that is in thy gates, that he may eat it; or thou mayest sell it unto an alien: for thou art an holy people unto the LORD thy God. Thou shalt not seethe a kid in his mother's milk.

181 *Exodus 22:31* - **Not to eat an animal which is torn or**

mauled, a treifah.

And ye shall be holy men unto me: neither shall ye eat any flesh that is torn of beasts in the field; ye shall cast it to the dogs.

182 *Deuteronomy 12:23 -* **Not to eat any limb taken from a living animal.**

Only be sure that thou eat not the blood: for the blood is the life; and thou mayest not eat the life with the flesh.

183 *Genesis 32:32 -* **Not to eat the sinew of the thigh-vein, (gid ha-nasheh).**

Therefore the children of Israel eat not of the sinew which shrank, which is upon the hollow of the thigh, unto this day: because he touched the hollow of Jacob's thigh in the sinew that shrank.

184 *Leviticus 7:26 -* **Not to eat blood.**

Moreover ye shall eat no manner of blood, whether it be of fowl or of beast, in any of your dwellings.

185 *Leviticus 7:23 -* **Not to eat certain types of fat of clean animal, chelev.**

Speak unto the children of Israel, saying, Ye shall eat no manner of fat, of ox, or of sheep, or of goat.

186 *Exodus 23:19 -* **Not to boil young male goat (meat) in its mother's milk.**

The first of the firstfruits of thy land thou shalt bring into the house of the LORD thy God. Thou shalt not seethe a kid in his mother's milk.

187 *Exodus 34:26 -* **Not to eat young male goat cooked in its mother's milk.**

The first of the firstfruits of thy land thou shalt bring unto the house of the LORD thy God. Thou shalt not seethe a kid in his mother's milk.

188 *Exodus 21:28 -* **Not to eat the flesh of a condemned and to**

be stoned ox.

If an ox gore a man or a woman, that they die: then the ox shall be surely stoned, and his flesh shall not be eaten; but the owner of the ox shall be quit.

189 *Leviticus 23:14 -* **Eat not bread made from grain of new crop, before bringing an offering.**

And ye shall eat neither bread, nor parched corn, nor green ears, until the selfsame day that ye have brought an offering unto your God: it shall be a statute for ever throughout your generations in all your dwellings.

190 *Leviticus 23:14 -* **Eat not roasted grain of new crop, before bringing an offering.**

And ye shall eat neither bread, nor parched corn, nor green ears, until the selfsame day that ye have brought an offering unto your God: it shall be a statute for ever throughout your generations in all your dwellings.

191 *Leviticus 23:14 -* **Eat not green ears of new crop, before bringing an offering.**

And ye shall eat neither bread, nor parched corn, nor green ears, until the selfsame day that ye have brought an offering unto your God: it shall be a statute for ever throughout your generations in all your dwellings.

192 *Leviticus 19:23 -* **Not to eat of the fruit of trees till the forth year, orlah .**

And when ye shall come into the land, and shall have planted all manner of trees for food, then ye shall count the fruit thereof as uncircumcised: three years shall it be as uncircumcised unto you: it shall not be eaten of.

193 *Deuteronomy 22:9 -* **Eat not growth of mixed vineyard planting, kilai hakerem.**

Thou shalt not sow thy vineyard with divers seeds: lest the fruit of thy seed which thou hast sown, and the fruit of thy vineyard, be defiled.

194 *Deuteronomy 32:38 -* **Not to use wine libations for idols, yayin nesach.**

Which did eat the fat of their sacrifices, and drank the wine of their drink offerings? let them rise up and help you, and be your protection.

195 *Deuteronomy 21:20 -* **No eating or drinking to excess, gluttony and drunkenness.**

And they shall say unto the elders of his city, This our son is stubborn and rebellious, he will not obey our voice; he is a glutton, and a drunkard.

196 *Leviticus 23:29 -* **Not to eat anything on Yom Kippur (Day of Atonement).**

For whatsoever soul it be that shall not be afflicted in that same day, he shall be cut off from among his people.

197 *Exodus 13:3 -* **Not to eat chametz, leaven, on Pesach (Passover).**

And Moses said unto the people, Remember this day, in which ye came out from Egypt, out of the house of bondage; for by strength of hand the LORD brought you out from this place: there shall no leavened bread be eaten.

198 *Exodus 13:7 -* **Not to eat an admixture of chametz / leaven on Pesach (Passover).**

Unleavened bread shall be eaten seven days; and there shall no leavened bread be seen with thee, neither shall there be leaven seen with thee in all thy quarters.

199 *Deuteronomy 16:3 -* **Not to eat chametz / leaven, after noon of 14th Nisan.**

Thou shalt eat no leavened bread with it; seven days shalt thou eat unleavened bread therewith, even the bread of affliction; for thou camest forth out of the land of Egypt in haste: that thou mayest remember the day when thou camest forth out of the land of Egypt all the days of thy life.

200 Exodus 13:7 - **No chametz / leaven may be seen in our homes during Pesach (Passover).**

Unleavened bread shall be eaten seven days; and there shall no leavened bread be seen with thee, neither shall there be leaven seen with thee in all thy quarters.

201 Exodus 12:19 - **Not to possess chametz / leaven, during Pesach (Passover).**

Seven days shall there be no leaven found in your houses: for whosoever eateth that which is leavened, even that soul shall be cut off from the congregation of Israel, whether he be a stranger, or born in the land.

NAZIRITES

202 Numbers 6:3 - **A Nazirite may not drink wine or any beverage from grapes.**

He shall separate himself from wine and strong drink, and shall drink no vinegar of wine, or vinegar of strong drink, neither shall he drink any liquor of grapes, nor eat moist grapes, or dried.

203 Numbers 6:3 - **A Nazirite may not eat fresh grapes.**

He shall separate himself from wine and strong drink, and shall drink no vinegar of wine, or vinegar of strong drink, neither shall he drink any liquor of grapes, nor eat moist grapes, or dried.

204 Numbers 6:3 - **A Nazirite may not eat dried grapes.**

He shall separate himself from wine and strong drink, and shall drink no vinegar of wine, or vinegar of strong drink, neither shall he drink any liquor of grapes, nor eat moist grapes, or dried.

205 Numbers 6:4 - **A Nazirite may not eat grape seeds / kernels.**

All the days of his separation shall he eat nothing that is made of the vine tree, from the kernels even to the husk.

206 *Numbers 6:4 -* **A Nazirite may not eat grape peels / husks.**

All the days of his separation shall he eat nothing that is made of the vine tree, from the kernels even to the husk.

207 *Numbers 6:7 -* **Nazirite may not rend himself tameh (unclean) for the dead.**

He shall not make himself unclean for his father, or for his mother, for his brother, or for his sister, when they die: because the consecration of his God is upon his head.

208 *Leviticus 21:11 -* **Nazirite must not become tameh entering house with corpse.**

Neither shall he go in to any dead body, nor defile himself for his father, or for his mother;

209 *Numbers 6:5 -* **A Nazirite must not shave his hair.**

All the days of the vow of his separation there shall no razor come upon his head: until the days be fulfilled, in the which he separateth himself unto the LORD, he shall be holy, and shall let the locks of the hair of his head grow.

AGRICULTURE

210 *Leviticus 23:22 -* **Reap not a whole field without leaving corners for poor.**

And when ye reap the harvest of your land, thou shalt not make clean riddance of the corners of thy field when thou reapest, neither shalt thou gather any gleaning of thy harvest: thou shalt leave them unto the poor, and to the stranger: I am the LORD your God.

211 *Leviticus 19:9 -* **Not to gather ears of grain that fell during harvesting.**

And when ye reap the harvest of your land, thou shalt not wholly reap the corners of thy field, neither shalt thou gather the gleanings of thy harvest.

212 *Leviticus 19:10 -* **Not to gather the misformed clusters of grapes.**

And thou shalt not glean thy vineyard, neither shalt thou gather every grape of thy vineyard; thou shalt leave them for the poor and stranger: I am the LORD your God.

213 *Leviticus 19:10 -* **Not to gather single fallen grapes during the vintage.**

And thou shalt not glean thy vineyard, neither shalt thou gather every grape of thy vineyard; thou shalt leave them for the poor and stranger: I am the LORD your God.

214 *Deuteronomy 24:19 -* **Not to return for a forgotten sheaf.**

When thou cuttest down thine harvest in thy field, and hast forgot a sheaf in the field, thou shalt not go again to fetch it: it shall be for the stranger, for the fatherless, and for the widow: that the LORD thy God may bless thee in all the work of thine hands.

215 *Leviticus 19:19 -* **Not to sow diverse kinds of seed in one field, kalayim.**

Ye shall keep my statutes. Thou shalt not let thy cattle gender with a diverse kind: thou shalt not sow thy field with mingled seed: neither shall a garment mingled of linen and woollen come upon thee.

216 *Deuteronomy 22:9 -* **Not to sow grain or vegetables in a vineyard.**

Thou shalt not sow thy vineyard with divers seeds: lest the fruit of thy seed which thou hast sown, and the fruit of thy vineyard, be defiled.

217 *Leviticus 19:19 -* **Not to crossbreed animals of different species.**

Ye shall keep my statutes. Thou shalt not let thy cattle gender with a diverse kind: thou shalt not sow thy field with mingled seed: neither shall a garment mingled of linen and woollen come upon thee.

218 *Deuteronomy 22:10 -* **Work not with two different kinds of animals together.**

Thou shalt not plow with an ox and an ass together.

219 *Deuteronomy 25:4 -* **Muzzle not animal working field to prevent from eating.**

Thou shalt not muzzle the ox when he treadeth out the corn.

220 *Leviticus 25:4 -* **Not to cultivate the soil in the 7th year, shemittah.**

But in the seventh year shall be a sabbath of rest unto the land, a sabbath for the LORD: thou shalt neither sow thy field, nor prune thy vineyard.

221 *Leviticus 25:4 -* **Not to prune the trees in the 7th year.**

But in the seventh year shall be a sabbath of rest unto the land, a sabbath for the LORD: thou shalt neither sow thy field, nor prune thy vineyard.

222 *Leviticus 25:5 -* **Reap not self-grown plant in 7th year as ordinary year.**

That which groweth of its own accord of thy harvest thou shalt not reap, neither gather the grapes of thy vine undressed: for it is a year of rest unto the land.

223 *Leviticus 25:5 -* **Gather not self-grown fruit in 7th year as ordinary year.**

That which groweth of its own accord of thy harvest thou shalt not reap, neither gather the grapes of thy vine undressed: for it is a year of rest unto the land.

224 *Leviticus 25:11 -* **Not to till the earth or prune trees in Jubilee year.**

A jubile shall that fiftieth year be unto you: ye shall not sow, neither reap that which groweth of itself in it, nor gather the grapes in it of thy vine undressed.

225 *Leviticus 25:11 -* **Reap not after-growths of Jubilee year as ordinary year.**

A jubile shall that fiftieth year be unto you: ye shall not sow, neither reap that which groweth of itself in it, nor gather the grapes in it of thy vine undressed.

226 *Leviticus 25:11 -* **Not to gather fruit in Jubilee year as in ordinary year.**

A jubile shall that fiftieth year be unto you: ye shall not sow, neither reap that which groweth of itself in it, nor gather the grapes in it of thy vine undressed.

227 *Leviticus 25:23 -* **Sell not one's Eretz Yisrael land holdings permanently.**

The land shall not be sold for ever: for the land is mine; for ye are strangers and sojourners with me.

228 *Leviticus 25:33 -* **Not to sell / change the open lands of the Levites.**

And if a man purchase of the Levites, then the house that was sold, and the city of his possession, shall go out in the year of jubile: for the houses of the cities of the Levites are their possession among the children of Israel.

229 *Deuteronomy 12:19 -* **Not to leave the Levites without support.**

Take heed to thyself that thou forsake not the Levite as long as thou livest upon the earth.

LOANS, BUSINESS, AND THE TREATMENT OF SLAVES

230 *Deuteronomy 15:2 -* **Not to demand payment of debts after 7th year Shmitah.**
And this is the manner of the release: Every creditor that lendeth ought unto his neighbour shall release it; he shall not exact it of his neighbour, or of his brother; because it is called the LORD'S release.

231 *Deuteronomy 15:9 -* **Not to refuse loan to poor because 7th year Shmitah is near.**
Beware that there be not a thought in thy wicked heart, saying, The seventh year, the year of release, is at hand; and thine eye be evil against thy poor brother, and thou givest him nought; and he cry unto the LORD against thee, and it be sin unto thee.

232 *Deuteronomy 15:7 -* **Not to deny charity to the poor.**
If there be among you a poor man of one of thy brethren within any of thy gates in thy land which the LORD thy God giveth thee, thou shalt not harden thine heart, nor shut thine hand from thy poor brother:

233 *Deuteronomy 15:13 -* **Not sending a Hebrew bondman away empty-handed.**
And when thou sendest him out free from thee, thou shalt not let him go away empty:

234 *Exodus 22:25 -* **Not demanding payment from a debtor known unable to pay.**
If thou lend money to any of my people that is poor by thee, thou shalt not be to him as an usurer, neither shalt thou lay upon him usury.

235 *Leviticus 25:37 -* **Not lending to another Jew at interest.**
Thou shalt not give him thy money upon usury, nor lend him thy

victuals for increase.

236 Deuteronomy 23:20 - **Not borrowing from another Jew at interest.**

Unto a stranger thou mayest lend upon usury; but unto thy brother thou shalt not lend upon usury: that the LORD thy God may bless thee in all that thou settest thine hand to in the land whither thou goest to possess it.

237 Exodus 22:25 - **Not participating in an agreement involving interest.**

If thou lend money to any of my people that is poor by thee, thou shalt not be to him as an usurer, neither shalt thou lay upon him usury.

238 Leviticus 19:13 - **Oppress not an employee by delaying paying his wages.**

Thou shalt not defraud thy neighbour, neither rob him: the wages of him that is hired shall not abide with thee all night until the morning.

239 Deuteronomy 24:10 - **Not taking a pledge from a debtor by force.**

When thou dost lend thy brother any thing, thou shalt not go into his house to fetch his pledge.

240 Deuteronomy 24:12 - **Not keeping a poor man's pledge when he needs it.**

And if the man be poor, thou shalt not sleep with his pledge:

241 Deuteronomy 24:17 - **Not taking any pledge from a widow.**

Thou shalt not pervert the judgment of the stranger, nor of the fatherless; nor take a widow's raiment to pledge:

242 Deuteronomy 24:6 - **Not taking one's business utensils in pledge.**

No man shall take the nether or the upper millstone to pledge: for he taketh a man's life to pledge.

243 *Exodus 20:13 - **Not abducting an Israelite.***
Thou shalt not kill.
244 *Leviticus 19:11 - **Not stealing.***
Ye shall not steal, neither deal falsely, neither lie one to another.
245 *Leviticus 19:13 - **Not robbing.***
Thou shalt not defraud thy neighbour, neither rob him: the wages of him that is hired shall not abide with thee all night until the morning.
246 *Deuteronomy 19:14 - **Not fraudulently altering land boundaries / landmarker.***
Thou shalt not remove thy neighbour's landmark, which they of old time have set in thine inheritance, which thou shalt inherit in the land that the LORD thy God giveth thee to possess it.
247 *Leviticus 19:13 - **Not usurping our debts and do not defraud.***
Thou shalt not defraud thy neighbour, neither rob him: the wages of him that is hired shall not abide with thee all night until the morning.
248 *Leviticus 19:11 - **Not repudiating debts, denying receipt of loan / deposit.***
Ye shall not steal, neither deal falsely, neither lie one to another.
249 *Leviticus 19:11 - **Not to swear falsely regarding another man's property.***
Ye shall not steal, neither deal falsely, neither lie one to another.
250 *Leviticus 25:14 - **Not wronging / deceiving one another in business.***
And if thou sell ought unto thy neighbour, or buyest ought of thy neighbour's hand, ye shall not oppress one another:
251 *Leviticus 25:17 - **Not wronging / misleading one another even verbally.***
Ye shall not therefore oppress one another; but thou shalt fear thy

God: for I am the LORD your God.

252 Exodus 22:21 - **Not harming the stranger among you verbally.**

Thou shalt neither vex a stranger, nor oppress him: for ye were strangers in the land of Egypt.

253 Exodus 22:21 - **Not injuring the stranger among you in business / trade.**

Thou shalt neither vex a stranger, nor oppress him: for ye were strangers in the land of Egypt.

254 Deuteronomy 23:15 - **Not handing over a slave who's fled to Israel.**

Thou shalt not deliver unto his master the servant which is escaped from his master unto thee:

255 Deuteronomy 23:16 - **Take no advantage of a slave who's fled to Israel.**

He shall dwell with thee, even among you, in that place which he shall choose in one of thy gates, where it liketh him best: thou shalt not oppress him.

256 Exodus 22:22 - **Not afflicting the orphans and widows.**

Thou shalt neither vex a stranger, nor oppress him: for ye were strangers in the land of Egypt.

257 Leviticus 25:39 - **Not employing a Hebrew bondman in degrading tasks.**

And if thy brother that dwelleth by thee be waxen poor, and be sold unto thee; thou shalt not compel him to serve as a bondservant:

258 Leviticus 25:42 - **Not selling a Hebrew bondman.**

For they are my servants, which I brought forth out of the land of Egypt: they shall not be sold as bondmen.

259 Leviticus 25:43 - **Not treating a Hebrew bondman cruelly.**

Thou shalt not rule over him with rigour; but shalt fear thy God.

260 Leviticus 25:53 - **Not allowing a heathen to mistreat a Hebrew bondman.**

And as a yearly hired servant shall he be with him: and the other shall not rule with rigour over him in thy sight.

261 Exodus 21:8 - **Not selling a Hebrew maidservant. and if you marry her...**

If she please not her master, who hath betrothed her to himself, then shall he let her be redeemed: to sell her unto a strange nation he shall have no power, seeing he hath dealt deceitfully with her.

262 Exodus 21:10 - **...withhold not: food, raiment, or conjugal rights.**

If he take him another wife; her food, her raiment, and her duty of marriage, shall he not diminish.

263 Deuteronomy 21:14 - **Not selling a captive woman.**

And it shall be, if thou have no delight in her, then thou shalt let her go whither she will; but thou shalt not sell her at all for money, thou shalt not make merchandise of her, because thou hast humbled her.

264 Deuteronomy 21:14 - **Not treating a captive woman as a slave.**

And it shall be, if thou have no delight in her, then thou shalt let her go whither she will; but thou shalt not sell her at all for money, thou shalt not make merchandise of her, because thou hast humbled her.

265 Exodus 20:17 - **Not coveting another man's possessions or property, etc.**

Thou shalt not covet thy neighbour's house, thou shalt not covet thy neighbour's wife, nor his manservant, nor his maidservant, nor his ox, nor his ass, nor any thing that is thy neighbour's.

266 Deuteronomy 5:21 - **Covet not another's possessions, even** *the desire forbidden.*

Neither shalt thou desire thy neighbour's wife, neither shalt thou covet thy neighbour's house, his field, or his manservant, or his maidservant, his ox, or his ass, or any thing that is thy neighbour's.

267 *Deuteronomy 23:25 -* **A worker is not to cut down standing grain during work.**

When thou comest into the standing corn of thy neighbour, then thou mayest pluck the ears with thine hand; but thou shalt not move a sickle unto thy neighbour's standing corn.

268 *Deuteronomy 23:24 -* **A hired laborer not to take more fruit than he can eat.**

When thou comest into thy neighbour's vineyard, then thou mayest eat grapes thy fill at thine own pleasure; but thou shalt not put any in thy vessel.

269 *Deuteronomy 22:3 -* **Not ignoring lost property to be returned to its owner.**

In like manner shalt thou do with his ass; and so shalt thou do with his raiment; and with all lost thing of thy brother's, which he hath lost, and thou hast found, shalt thou do likewise: thou mayest not hide thyself.

270 *Exodus 23:5 -* **Refuse not to help man or animal collapsing with burden.**

If thou see the ass of him that hateth thee lying under his burden, and wouldest forbear to help him, thou shalt surely help with him.

271 *Leviticus 19:35 -* **Not cheating or defrauding with measurements and weights.**

Ye shall do no unrighteousness in judgment, in meteyard, in weight, or in measure.

272 *Deuteronomy 25:13 -* **Not to possess false or inaccurate**

weights and measures.

Thou shalt not have in thy bag divers weights, a great and a small.

JUSTICE

273 *Leviticus 19:15 -* ***A Judge is not to commit unrighteousness.***

Ye shall do no unrighteousness in judgment: thou shalt not respect the person of the poor, nor honour the person of the mighty: but in righteousness shalt thou judge thy neighbour.

274 *Exodus 23:8 -* ***A Judge is not to accept bribes / gifts from litigants.***

And thou shalt take no gift: for the gift blindeth the wise, and perverteth the words of the righteous.

275 *Leviticus 19:15 -* ***A Judge is not to favor (be partial to) a litigant.***

Ye shall do no unrighteousness in judgment: thou shalt not respect the person of the poor, nor honour the person of the mighty: but in righteousness shalt thou judge thy neighbour.

276 *Deuteronomy 1:17 -* ***Judge not avoid justice being in fear of wicked person.***

Ye shall not respect persons in judgment; but ye shall hear the small as well as the great; ye shall not be afraid of the face of man; for the judgment is God's: and the cause that is too hard for you, bring it unto me, and I will hear it.

277 *Leviticus 19:15 -* ***A Judge not to decide in favor of poor man, out of pity.***

Ye shall do no unrighteousness in judgment: thou shalt not respect the person of the poor, nor honour the person of the mighty: but in righteousness shalt thou judge thy neighbour.

278 Exodus 23:6 - **A Judge is not to discriminate against the poor.**

Thou shalt not wrest the judgment of thy poor in his cause.

279 Deuteronomy 19:13 - **Judge not to pity one who killed or caused loss of limb.**

Thine eye shall not pity him, but thou shalt put away the guilt of innocent blood from Israel, that it may go well with thee.

280 Deuteronomy 24:17 - **A Judge not perverting justice due strangers or orphans.**

Thou shalt not pervert the judgment of the stranger, nor of the fatherless; nor take a widow's raiment to pledge:

281 Exodus 23:1 - **Judge not to hear one litigant in absence of the other.**

Thou shalt not raise a false report: put not thine hand with the wicked to be an unrighteous witness.

282 Exodus 23:2 - **Court may not convict by majority of one in capital case.**

Thou shalt not follow a multitude to do evil; neither shalt thou speak in a cause to decline after many to wrest judgment:

283 Exodus 23:2 - **Judge accept not colleague's opinion, unless sure right.**

Thou shalt not follow a multitude to do evil; neither shalt thou speak in a cause to decline after many to wrest judgment:

284 Deuteronomy 1:17 - **Not appointing an unlearned judge ignorant of the Torah.**

Ye shall not respect persons in judgment; but ye shall hear the small as well as the great; ye shall not be afraid of the face of man; for the judgment is God's: and the cause that is too hard for you, bring it unto me, and I will hear it.

285 Exodus 20:16 - **Not bearing false witness.**

Thou shalt not bear false witness against thy neighbour.

286 *Exodus 23:1 - **A Judge is not to receive a wicked man's testimony.***

Thou shalt not raise a false report: put not thine hand with the wicked to be an unrighteous witness.

287 *Deuteronomy 24:16 - **A Judge receive not testimony from litigant's relatives.***

The fathers shall not be put to death for the children, neither shall the children be put to death for the fathers: every man shall be put to death for his own sin.

288 *Deuteronomy 19:15 - **Not convicting on the testimony of a single witness.***

One witness shall not rise up against a man for any iniquity, or for any sin, in any sin that he sinneth: at the mouth of two witnesses, or at the mouth of three witnesses, shall the matter be established.

289 *Exodus 20:13 - **Not murdering a human being.***

Thou shalt not kill.

290 *Exodus 23:7 - **No conviction based on circumstantial evidence alone.***

Keep thee far from a false matter; and the innocent and righteous slay thou not: for I will not justify the wicked.

291 *Numbers 35:30 - **A witness must not sit as a Judge in capital cases.***

Whoso killeth any person, the murderer shall be put to death by the mouth of witnesses: but one witness shall not testify against any person to cause him to die.

292 *Numbers 35:12 - **Not killing a murderer without trial and conviction.***

And they shall be unto you cities for refuge from the avenger; that the manslayer die not, until he stand before the congregation in judgment.

293 *Deuteronomy 25:12 -* **Not to pity or spare the life of a pursuer.**
Then thou shalt cut off her hand, thine eye shall not pity her.
294 *Deuteronomy 22:26 -* **Not punishing a person for a sin committed under duress.**
But unto the damsel thou shalt do nothing; there is in the damsel no sin worthy of death: for as when a man riseth against his neighbour, and slayeth him, even so is this matter:
295 *Numbers 35:31 -* **Not accepting ransom from an unwitting murderer.**
Moreover ye shall take no satisfaction for the life of a murderer, which is guilty of death: but he shall be surely put to death.
296 *Numbers 35:32 -* **Not accepting a ransom from a wilful murderer.**
And ye shall take no satisfaction for him that is fled to the city of his refuge, that he should come again to dwell in the land, until the death of the priest.
297 *Leviticus 19:16 -* **Hesitate not to save life of another person in danger.**
Thou shalt not go up and down as a talebearer among thy people: neither shalt thou stand against the blood of thy neighbour: I am the LORD.
298 *Deuteronomy 22:8 -* **Not leaving obstacles on public or private domain.**
When thou buildest a new house, then thou shalt make a battlement for thy roof, that thou bring not blood upon thine house, if any man fall from thence.
299 *Leviticus 19:14 -* **Not misleading another by giving wrong advice.**
Thou shalt not curse the deaf, nor put a stumblingblock before the blind, but shalt fear thy God: I am the LORD.

*300 Deuteronomy 25:2,3 - **Inflict not more than assigned number lashes to guilty.***
And it shall be, if the wicked man be worthy to be beaten, that the judge shall cause him to lie down, and to be beaten before his face, according to his fault, by a certain number. Forty stripes he may give him, and not exceed: lest, if he should exceed, and beat him above these with many stripes, then thy brother should seem vile unto thee.

*301 Leviticus 19:16 - **Not to tell tales.***
Thou shalt not go up and down as a talebearer among thy people: neither shalt thou stand against the blood of thy neighbour: I am the LORD.

*302 Leviticus 19:17 - **Not to bear hatred in your heart toward your brethren.***
Thou shalt not hate thy brother in thine heart: thou shalt in any wise rebuke thy neighbour, and not suffer sin upon him.

*303 Leviticus 19:17 - **Not to put one another to shame.***
Thou shalt not hate thy brother in thine heart: thou shalt in any wise rebuke thy neighbour, and not suffer sin upon him.

*304 Leviticus 19:18 - **Not to take vengeance on another.***
Thou shalt not avenge, nor bear any grudge against the children of thy people, but thou shalt love thy neighbour as thyself: I am the LORD.

*305 Leviticus 19:18 - **Not to bear a grudge.***
Thou shalt not avenge, nor bear any grudge against the children of thy people, but thou shalt love thy neighbour as thyself: I am the LORD.

*306 Deuteronomy 22:6 - **Not to take entire bird's nest, mother and her young.***
If a bird's nest chance to be before thee in the way in any tree, or on the ground, whether they be young ones, or eggs, and the dam

sitting upon the young, or upon the eggs, thou shalt not take the dam with the young:

307 *Leviticus 13:33* - **Not to shave a leprous scall.**

He shall be shaven, but the scall shall he not shave; and the priest shall shut up him that hath the scall seven days more:

308 *Deuteronomy 24:8* - **Not to cut or cauterize (remove) other signs of leprosy.**

Take heed in the plague of leprosy, that thou observe diligently, and do according to all that the priests the Levites shall teach you: as I commanded them, so ye shall observe to do.

309 *Deuteronomy 21:4* - **Plow not a valley where slain body found, eglah arufah.**

And the elders of that city shall bring down the heifer unto a rough valley, which is neither eared nor sown, and shall strike off the heifer's neck there in the valley:

310 *Exodus 22:18* - **Not permitting a witch / sorcerer to live.**

Thou shalt not suffer a witch to live.

311 *Deuteronomy 24:5* - **Take not bridegroom from home in first year of marriage.**

When a man hath taken a new wife, he shall not go out to war, neither shall he be charged with any business: but he shall be free at home one year, and shall cheer up his wife which he hath taken.

312 *Deuteronomy 17:11* - **Not to differ from or disobey the Cohanim and the Judge.**

According to the sentence of the law which they shall teach thee, and according to the judgment which they shall tell thee, thou shalt do: thou shalt not decline from the sentence which they shall shew thee, to the right hand, nor to the left.

313 *Deuteronomy 12:32* - **Not to add to the Mitzvot / commandments of Torah.**

What thing soever I command you, observe to do it: thou shalt not add thereto, nor diminish from it.

*314 Deuteronomy 12:32 - **Not to detract from the Mitzvot / commandments of Torah.***

What thing soever I command you, observe to do it: thou shalt not add thereto, nor diminish from it.

*315 Exodus 22:28 - **Not to curse a judge.***

Thou shalt not revile the gods, nor curse the ruler of thy people.

*316 Exodus 22:28 - **Not to curse a ruler.***

Thou shalt not revile the gods, nor curse the ruler of thy people.

*317 Leviticus 19:14 - **Not to curse any Jew.***

Thou shalt not curse the deaf, nor put a stumblingblock before the blind, but shalt fear thy God: I am the LORD.

*318 Exodus 21:17 - **Not cursing parents.***

And he that curseth his father, or his mother, shall surely be put to death.

*319 Exodus 21:15 - **Not to strike parents.***

And he that smiteth his father, or his mother, shall be surely put to death.

*320 Exodus 20:10 - **Not to work on Shabbat.***

But the seventh day is the sabbath of the LORD thy God: in it thou shalt not do any work, thou, nor thy son, nor thy daughter, thy manservant, nor thy maidservant, nor thy cattle, nor thy stranger that is within thy gates:

*321 Exodus 16:29 - **Not to walk beyond permitted limits, eruv, on Shabbat.***

See, for that the LORD hath given you the sabbath, therefore he giveth you on the sixth day the bread of two days; abide ye every man in his place, let no man go out of his place on the seventh day.

*322 Exodus 35:3 - **Not to inflict punishment on the Shabbat.***

Ye shall kindle no fire throughout your habitations upon the sabbath day.

323 *Exodus 12:16 -* **Not to work on the first day of Pesach (Passover).**

And in the first day there shall be an holy convocation, and in the seventh day there shall be an holy convocation to you; no manner of work shall be done in them, save that which every man must eat, that only may be done of you.

324 *Exodus 12:16 -* **Not to work on the seventh day of Pesach (Passover).**

And in the first day there shall be an holy convocation, and in the seventh day there shall be an holy convocation to you; no manner of work shall be done in them, save that which every man must eat, that only may be done of you.

325 *Leviticus 23:21 -* **Not to work on Shavuot (Pentecost).**

And ye shall proclaim on the selfsame day, that it may be an holy convocation unto you: ye shall do no servile work therein: it shall be a statute for ever in all your dwellings throughout your generations.

326 *Leviticus 23:25 -* **Not to work on Rosh HaShannah (Head of Year).**

Ye shall do no servile work therein: but ye shall offer an offering made by fire unto the LORD.

327 *Leviticus 23:35 -* **Not to work on the first day of Sukkot (Booths).**

On the first day shall be an holy convocation: ye shall do no servile work therein.

328 *Leviticus 23:36 -* **Work not 8th-day / Shemini-Atzeret, (after Hoshana Rabba).**

Seven days ye shall offer an offering made by fire unto the LORD: on the eighth day shall be an holy convocation unto you;

and ye shall offer an offering made by fire unto the LORD: it is a solemn assembly; and ye shall do no servile work therein.

329 *Leviticus 23:28 -* **Not to work on Yom Kippur (Day of Atonement).**

And ye shall do no work in that same day: for it is a day of atonement, to make an atonement for you before the LORD your God.

INCEST AND OTHER FORBIDDEN RELATIONSHIPS

330 *Leviticus 18:7 -* **No relations with one's mother.**
The nakedness of thy father, or the nakedness of thy mother, shalt thou not uncover: she is thy mother; thou shalt not uncover her nakedness.

331 *Leviticus 18:8 -* **No relations with one's father's wife.**
The nakedness of thy father's wife shalt thou not uncover: it is thy father's nakedness.

332 *Leviticus 18:9 -* **No relations with one's sister.**
The nakedness of thy sister, the daughter of thy father, or daughter of thy mother, whether she be born at home, or born abroad, even their nakedness thou shalt not uncover.

333 *Leviticus 18:11 -* **No relations with step-sister.**
The nakedness of thy father's wife's daughter, begotten of thy father, she is thy sister, thou shalt not uncover her nakedness.

334 *Leviticus 18:10 -* **No relations with one's son's daughter.**
The nakedness of thy son's daughter, or of thy daughter's daughter, even their nakedness thou shalt not uncover: for theirs is thine own nakedness.

335 *Leviticus 18:10 -* **No relations with one's daughter's daughter.**
The nakedness of thy son's daughter, or of thy daughter's

daughter, even their nakedness thou shalt not uncover: for theirs is thine own nakedness.

*336 Leviticus 18:10 - **No relations with one's daughter.***
The nakedness of thy son's daughter, or of thy daughter's daughter, even their nakedness thou shalt not uncover: for theirs is thine own nakedness.

*337 Leviticus 18:17 - **No relations with a woman and her daughter.***
Thou shalt not uncover the nakedness of a woman and her daughter, neither shalt thou take her son's daughter, or her daughter's daughter, to uncover her nakedness; for they are her near kinswomen: it is wickedness.

*338 Leviticus 18:17 - **No relations with a woman and her son's daughter.***
Thou shalt not uncover the nakedness of a woman and her daughter, neither shalt thou take her son's daughter, or her daughter's daughter, to uncover her nakedness; for they are her near kinswomen: it is wickedness.

*339 Leviticus 18:17 - **No relations with a woman and her daughter's daughter.***
Thou shalt not uncover the nakedness of a woman and her daughter, neither shalt thou take her son's daughter, or her daughter's daughter, to uncover her nakedness; for they are her near kinswomen: it is wickedness.

*340 Leviticus 18:12 - **No relations with one's father's sister.***
Thou shalt not uncover the nakedness of thy father's sister: she is thy father's near kinswoman.

*341 Leviticus 18:13 - **No relations with one's mother's sister.***
Thou shalt not uncover the nakedness of thy mother's sister: for she is thy mother's near kinswoman.

*342 Leviticus 18:14 - **No relations with wife of father's brother.***

Thou shalt not uncover the nakedness of thy father's brother, thou shalt not approach to his wife: she is thine aunt.

343** Leviticus 18:15 - **No relations with one's son's wife.

Thou shalt not uncover the nakedness of thy daughter in law: she is thy son's wife; thou shalt not uncover her nakedness.

344** Leviticus 18:16 - **No relations with brother's wife.

Thou shalt not uncover the nakedness of thy brother's wife: it is thy brother's nakedness.

345** Leviticus 18:18 - **No relations with sister of wife, during wife's life.

Neither shalt thou take a wife to her sister, to vex her, to uncover her nakedness, beside the other in her life time.

346** Leviticus 18:19 - **No relations with a menstruant.

Also thou shalt not approach unto a woman to uncover her nakedness, as long as she is put apart for her uncleanness.

347** Leviticus 18:20 - **No relations with another man's wife.

Moreover thou shalt not lie carnally with thy neighbour's wife, to defile thyself with her.

348** Leviticus 18:23 - **Men may not lie with beasts.

Neither shalt thou lie with any beast to defile thyself therewith: neither shall any woman stand before a beast to lie down thereto: it is confusion.

349** Leviticus 18:23 - **Women may not lie with beasts.

Neither shalt thou lie with any beast to defile thyself therewith: neither shall any woman stand before a beast to lie down thereto: it is confusion.

350** Leviticus 18:22 - **A man may not lie carnally with another man.

Thou shalt not lie with mankind, as with womankind: it is abomination.

351** Leviticus 18:7 - **A man may not lie carnally with his father.

The nakedness of thy father, or the nakedness of thy mother, shalt thou not uncover: she is thy mother; thou shalt not uncover her nakedness.

352 *Leviticus 18:14 -* **A man may not lie carnally with his father's brother.**

Thou shalt not uncover the nakedness of thy father's brother, thou shalt not approach to his wife: she is thine aunt.

353 *Leviticus 18:6 -* **Not to be intimate with a kinswoman.**

None of you shall approach to any that is near of kin to him, to uncover their nakedness: I am the LORD.

354 *Deuteronomy 23:2 –* **A mamzer may not have relations with a Jewess.**

A bastard shall not enter into the congregation of the LORD; even to his tenth generation shall he not enter into the congregation of the LORD.

355 *Deuteronomy 23:17 -* **No relations (harlotry) with a woman outside marriage.**

There shall be no whore of the daughters of Israel, nor a sodomite of the sons of Israel.

356 *Deuteronomy 24:4 -* **Remarry not your divorced wife after she has remarried.**

Her former husband, which sent her away, may not take her again to be his wife, after that she is defiled; for that is abomination before the LORD: and thou shalt not cause the land to sin, which the LORD thy God giveth thee for an inheritance.

357 *Deuteronomy 25:5 -* **Childless widow marry none except late husbands brother.**

If brethren dwell together, and one of them die, and have no child, the wife of the dead shall not marry without unto a stranger: her husband's brother shall go in unto her, and take her to him to wife, and perform the duty of an husband's brother unto her.

358 *Deuteronomy 22:29 -* **Divorce not wife, that he has to marry after raping her.**

Then the man that lay with her shall give unto the damsel's father fifty shekels of silver, and she shall be his wife; because he hath humbled her, he may not put her away all his days.

359 *Deuteronomy 22:19 -* **Divorce not wife, after falsely slandering her.**

And they shall amerce him in an hundred shekels of silver, and give them unto the father of the damsel, because he hath brought up an evil name upon a virgin of Israel: and she shall be his wife; he may not put her away all his days.

360 *Deuteronomy 23:1 -* **Man unable of procreation (eunuch) not to marry Jewess.**

He that is wounded in the stones, or hath his privy member cut off, shall not enter into the congregation of the LORD.

361 *Leviticus 22:24 -* **Not to castrate a man or beast.**

Ye shall not offer unto the LORD that which is bruised, or crushed, or broken, or cut; neither shall ye make any offering thereof in your land.

THE MONARCHY

362 *Deuteronomy 17:15 -* **Not appointing a king who is not of the seed of Israel.**

Thou shalt in any wise set him king over thee, whom the LORD thy God shall choose: one from among thy brethren shalt thou set king over thee: thou mayest not set a stranger over thee, which is not thy brother.

363 *Deuteronomy 17:16 -* **A king not to accumulate an excess number of horses.**

But he shall not multiply horses to himself, nor cause the people to return to Egypt, to the end that he should multiply horses: forasmuch as the LORD hath said unto you, Ye shall henceforth return no more that way.

*364 Deuteronomy 17:17 - **A king not taking many wives.***

Neither shall he multiply wives to himself, that his heart turn not away: neither shall he greatly multiply to himself silver and gold.

*365 Deuteronomy 17:17 - **A king may not amass great personal wealth.***

Neither shall he multiply wives to himself, that his heart turn not away: neither shall he greatly multiply to himself silver and gold.

- END LIST -

Resources:

www.jewfaq.org

www.Chabad.org

www.jewishvirtuallibrary.org

www.judaism.about.com